MW00668880

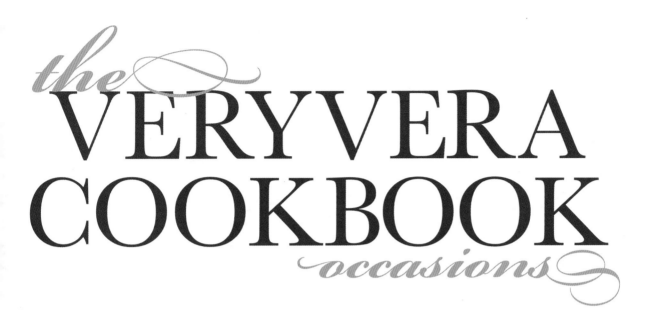

the VERYVERA COOKBOOK occasions

VERA STEWART

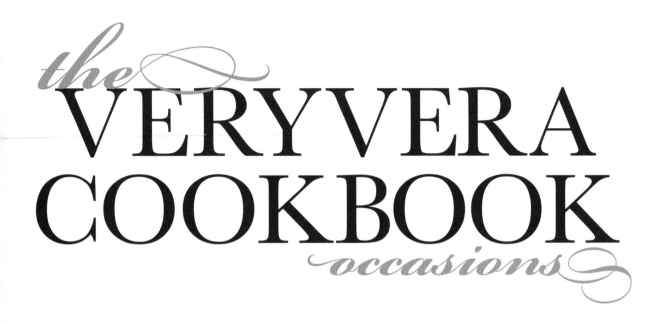

the VERYVERA COOKBOOK occasions

VERA STEWART

PHOTOGRAPHY BY PETER FRANK EDWARDS

ILLUSTRATIONS BY KAT McCALL

STORY FARM

WINTER PARK · MIAMI · SANTA BARBARA

The VeryVera Cookbook: Occasions

Copyright © 2023 by Vera Stewart

Photographs copyright © 2023 by Peter Frank Edwards

Illustrations copyright © 2023 by Kat McCall

ISBN: 978-1-7376046-6-2

Library of Congress Cataloging in Publication data available upon request.

Published in the United States by Story Farm

www.story-farm.com

VERYVERA ENTERPRISES

Project Manager Rachel Musgrove

Culinary Director Donna Nail

Culinary Assistant Haleigh Newman

Recipe Testers Christina Cannon, Melissa Carden, Debbie Tamplin

STORY FARM

Editorial Director Ashley Fraxedas

Art Director Lauren Eggert

Production Director Tina Dahl

Copy Editors Laura Paquette, Karen Cakebread

Indexer Amy Hall

Photography Peter Frank Edwards

Photography Assistant Nick Milak

Printed in China by Crash Paper of Playa Del Rey, California

First printing, April 2023

10 9 8 7 6 5 4 3 2 1

Cover images by Peter Frank Edwards

www.pfephoto.com

To all the staff, both young and old,
that have cared for our VeryVera
with love & devotion.

TABLE OF *contents*

It all started with polishing silver.

I was three years old when I first understood the difference between everyday life and special occasions. Everyday life meant familiar meals and well-worn tableware. But special occasions? That meant seasonal favorites coming out of our kitchen and, first things first, polishing the silver.

The silver cabinet held a place of prominence in our home. Even as a young girl, I knew it meant being "fancy." Every piece in that cabinet had a story behind it, from the hand-engraved trays that were wedding gifts to my mother and daddy to the coffee urn that was buried in the creek when Sherman came through Georgia. My favorite was my grandmother's silver cake stand with its lacy filigree. This treasured piece always appeared on my birthday topped with a German chocolate cake. When my mother started pulling items from the silver cabinet and sat down with the jar of polish, I knew a special occasion was on the way. Enlisting my help, Mama taught me how to wet the sponge,

dab a smear of the polish and use some elbow grease, making sure to get it in all the crevices, even if you had to use a toothbrush. A lot of work, yes, but it meant something. Special occasions deserved that sort of attention. And I loved helping make them happen.

I guess you could say my career path was set from an early age. I love everything about event planning, from the food preparation to the décor and all the logistics in between. I couldn't be more grateful for getting to do what I love. In planning the first photo shoot for this book, I started gathering pieces from my own silver cabinet—and from under the beds and all the closets. I was a bit daunted as I laid it all out. I envisioned spending hours and hours polishing every piece to make it perfect. That's when our photographer, Peter Frank Edwards, asked: "Why would you ever do that?" A great question that made me realize—these pieces, as they are, tell my family's story.

A lot of reminiscing went into this book. The chapters take you through each season and the special occasions that coincide. With Spring comes The Masters Golf Tournament in Augusta, an event that has been the core of my catering career. Summer reminds me of the Stewart family reunion and all the recipes I looked forward to savoring, almost as much as seeing the aunt or cousin that made each dish. Halloween makes me realize how quickly my grandchildren are growing! And Winter, of course, brings our favorite time of year, Christmas. I could have written an entire book with just my family's holiday recipes.

As you read through this book, I hope you find inspiration for your own special occasions.

CHAPTER 1

Spring Flings

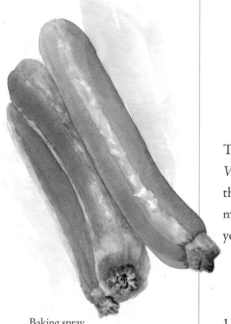

ZUCCHINI BREAD

{MAKES 2 (8 X 4-INCH) LOAVES}

This recipe is in my Top 10! I made this in Season 1 of *The Very-Vera Show*. The touch of lavender adds the slight unexpected twist that will keep you wanting another slice…good thing this recipe makes two loaves! If needed, the bread can be frozen and saved for your next occasion.

Baking spray

4 large eggs, at room temperature

2 cups granulated sugar

1 cup vegetable oil

3 cups all-purpose flour

2 teaspoons baking soda

1 teaspoon baking powder

1 teaspoon ground cinnamon

1½ teaspoons kosher salt

2 cups shredded zucchini (do not peel and use the large side of a box grater)

1½ tablespoons pure vanilla extract

1 cup chopped walnuts

½ teaspoon dried lavender buds

1. Preheat the oven to 350°F and prepare two 8 x 4-inch loaf pans with baking spray.

2. Blend the first three ingredients thoroughly in a large mixing bowl.

3. In a separate mixing bowl, sift together the flour, baking soda, baking powder, cinnamon, and salt.

4. Add the dry ingredients to the wet ingredients and mix.

5. Add in the zucchini, vanilla extract, walnuts, and lavender buds, and mix until just combined.

6. Pour the batter into two greased loaf pans.

7. Place in the oven and bake for 45 to 55 minutes, or until a wooden skewer inserted in the middle comes out clean.

8. Remove the loaf pans from the oven and cool on wire racks.

PREP TIME: 20 minutes | BAKE TIME: 45-55 minutes

VEGETABLE TART

{ S E R V E S 8 T O 1 2 }

In the South, a colorful tart is the introduction to spring menus. This recipe is the perfect excuse to head to your local farmers market and pick out all the fresh ingredients. Depending on the occasion, you choose how to serve this dish: slice into triangles or cut smaller squares for the perfect bite.

---

1. Preheat the oven to 450°F and prepare a sheet pan with cooking spray. Place the puff pastry on the prepared sheet pan and prick several times with a fork.

2. Pre-bake the puff pastry crust for 6 minutes. Remove from the oven, set aside, and let cool. Turn the oven down to 425°F.

3. Toss all the vegetables with minced garlic and olive oil. Spread the vegetables on a rimmed sheet pan and sprinkle with salt and pepper. Place in the oven and roast for about 20 minutes. Remove from the oven and set aside. Turn the oven down to 350°F.

4. In a separate bowl, mix together the chopped artichokes, mayonnaise, and cheeses. Add in the roasted vegetables and mix well.

5. Spread the mixture over the cooled pastry crust. Bake for approximately 20 minutes. Raise the oven temperature to 375°F and bake for another 6 to 7 minutes, or until the crust has browned and the cheese is bubbly.

6. Serve warm and enjoy!

PREP TIME: 20 minutes | BAKE TIME: 50 minutes

Cooking spray

1 sheet Pepperidge Farm® puff pastry

½ cup sliced yellow squash

½ cup sliced zucchini

½ cup sliced Vidalia onion

½ cup sliced Roma tomato

¼ cup red bell pepper strips

¼ cup yellow bell pepper strips

2 teaspoons minced garlic

2 tablespoons extra-virgin olive oil

Kosher salt, to taste

Freshly ground black pepper, to taste

7 ounces canned artichokes, drained

½ cup mayonnaise

1 cup shredded Gruyère cheese

¼ cup shredded cheddar cheese

½ cup shredded Asiago cheese, plus more for topping

SOUR CREAM BANANA CAKE

{MAKES 1 LARGE BUNDT CAKE }

Although this recipe uses a cake mix as the base, the extra added ingredients elevate this cake to something you'll want to make again and again. The best part is you can make it in a hurry and knock out several to give to the neighbors. Tint the icing Easter colors to make it festive. And if there is any leftover cake the next day, no one will know if you decide to eat it for breakfast.

CAKE

Baking spray

1 (15.25-ounce) box yellow cake mix

1 (3.4-ounce) box French vanilla instant pudding

3 large eggs, at room temperature

½ cup sour cream

¼ cup vegetable oil

2 large ripe bananas

⅛ teaspoon ground mace

FROSTING

3 ounces cream cheese, at room temperature

3 tablespoons unsalted butter, at room temperature

½ teaspoon freshly grated orange peel

1 tablespoon freshly squeezed orange juice

1 ½ cups confectioners' sugar

Food coloring (optional)

Banana slices brushed with lemon juice, or orange zest for garnish

1. Preheat the oven to 350°F and prepare a 12-cup Bundt pan with baking spray.

2. Mix the cake mix and pudding mix in a large bowl of a stand mixer, using the paddle attachment. Add in the eggs, one at a time, mixing well after each addition.

3. Add in the sour cream, oil, bananas, and mace. Mix on low to blend and then beat at medium speed for 5 minutes.

4. Pour the batter into the prepared Bundt pan, and tap the pan on the counter so there are no bubbles. Bake for 50 minutes, or until a toothpick inserted in the middle of the cake comes out clean.

5. Cool for 10 to 15 minutes in the pan, then invert the Bundt pan onto a wire rack and flip the cake out to cool completely.

6. While the cake is cooling, prepare the frosting.

7. Beat the butter and cream cheese in the bowl of a stand mixer fitted with the paddle attachment until well combined.

8. Add in the orange peel and orange juice, and beat to combine. Add the confectioners' sugar slowly to the cream cheese mixture. Mix until the frosting comes together and fully combines. (Add a few drops of food coloring at this point, if desired.)

9. Frost the cooled Bundt cake and top with banana slices, if desired, to garnish.

PREP TIME: 15-20 minutes | BAKE TIME: 50 minutes

DEVILED EGGS

{ MAKES 24 }

Sometimes the hardest part of deviled eggs is hard-cooking and peeling them. I place my eggs in a large saucepan and cover with water (1 inch over eggs). Heat to high and allow the water to boil. Turn off the heat immediately, cover the pot, and let sit for 20 minutes. Rinse with cold water and peel. The secret ingredients…famous Durkee® sauce and Wickles® pickles!

---

1. Slice the eggs in half lengthwise. Pop the yellow yolks into a small bowl and mash with a fork until fine.

2. Add in the Durkee® sauce, mayonnaise, mustard, and pickles. Stir well until it is completely blended. Add more mayonnaise and pickles, if needed, and salt and pepper, to taste.

3. Using a piping bag or a teaspoon, fill each egg-white half with the egg yolk mixture.

4. Cover and store in the refrigerator until ready to eat.

5. Before serving, top with candied bacon and paprika, if using.

PREP TIME: 10 minutes | SHELF LIFE: 4 to 5 days in the refrigerator

12 large eggs, hard-cooked and peeled

2 teaspoons Durkee® sauce

2 tablespoons Hellmann's® mayonnaise, or more to taste

1 teaspoon French's® yellow mustard

1 heaping tablespoon Wickles® pickles, chopped

Kosher salt, to taste

Freshly ground black pepper, to taste

½ cup Maple-Candied Bacon (page 48), to garnish

Paprika, optional

SUE'S CARROT
SANDWICHES

{MAKES 40 TEA SANDWICHES}

Sue Stewart was my mother-in-law. She taught me so much about entertaining, cooking, and housekeeping. One of my first memories of being at her home was this petite bite-sized sandwich. Need to feed a crowd with appetizers? This is the one!

———

½ pound carrots (about 2 to 3), peeled

¼ cup ground pecans

6 tablespoons Hellmann's® mayonnaise, plus more for spreading

¼ teaspoon garlic salt, plus more to taste

½ loaf white sandwich bread

1. Roughly chop the carrots and place in a blender. Cover carrots with water and blend until smooth.

2. Pour the blended carrots into a colander and squeeze out as much excess water as possible.

3. Transfer to a large bowl and mix in the ground pecans, mayonnaise, and garlic salt.

4. Trim the crust from the slices of bread and roll out each slice of bread with a rolling pin until very flat.

5. Spread a thin layer of mayonnaise on each slice and top with a thin layer of the carrot mixture.

6. Roll up like a jelly roll and cut into ½-inch pinwheels. Cover the sandwiches with a damp paper towel as you work, to keep them moist. Keep covered with the damp paper towels in the refrigerator until ready to serve. The sandwiches will hold up well for up to 24 hours.

PREP TIME: 20 minutes

CHICKEN ARTICHOKE SPREAD

{SERVES 10 TO 12 PEOPLE AS AN APPETIZER PORTION}

Chicken Artichoke Spread can be a great way to showcase spread in a likeness that typically is represented with cheeseballs. In this case for Easter, bite-sized eggs can be nestled into alfalfa sprouts and served with crackers. A larger version can be made to represent a bigger egg and can be presented like the Golden Egg to steal the show on an appetizer table. Use your imagination for whatever the occasion may be.

---

1. In a large bowl, combine all ingredients and mix thoroughly. The mixture will be chunky.

2. Cover the bowl with plastic wrap and place in the refrigerator to chill.

3. While the mixture is in the refrigerator, make the green onion garnish. To blanch the green onion stems, place in boiling water for 2 to 4 minutes, or until they turn bright green. Immediately place in ice water to stop the cooking process. Transfer to paper towels to drain and dry the stems.

4. Once the mixture is chilled, shape into a large Easter egg or smaller versions that can be nestled like a bird's nest. For the smaller eggs, use about a tablespoon of the mixture rolled into small egg shapes. Create a board or a platter to look like an Easter tablescape.

5. To garnish, press the green onion stems into the sides of the larger egg and fluff up the alfalfa sprouts around the eggs. Serve with crackers or toasted French baguette slices.

Note: This will last in the refrigerator for 5 days.

PREP TIME: 30 minutes

1½ cups shredded rotisserie chicken

1 cup shaved Parmesan cheese

8 ounces cream cheese, softened

2 tablespoons mayonnaise

7 ounces canned artichoke hearts, drained and diced

½ cup finely chopped pecans

2 green onions, minced

½ tablespoon freshly squeezed lemon juice

¼ teaspoon kosher salt

½ teaspoon Lawry's® Seasoned Pepper (Colorful Coarse Ground Blend)

GARNISH

1 (4-ounce) container alfalfa sprouts

Blanched green onion stems, as needed

French baguette

GREEN BEAN ALMONDINE

{ S E R V E S   4 }

A simple and delicious side dish that is easy to throw together at the last minute. My husband says, "Don't put nuts in my food!" If your husband is the same way, just leave them off. The balsamic glaze, however, is a delicious extra garnish.

1 pound green beans, stems trimmed off

4 tablespoons extra-virgin olive oil

Kosher salt, to taste

Freshly ground black pepper, to taste

½ cup sliced almonds, toasted*

Balsamic glaze (optional), to garnish

1. Preheat the oven to 425°F and line a baking sheet with parchment paper or aluminum foil.

2. Spread the green beans in an even layer on the prepared baking sheet.

3. Drizzle the green beans with olive oil and sprinkle generously with kosher salt and freshly ground black pepper to taste. Toss to coat everything evenly.

4. Place on the center rack in the oven and roast for about 8 minutes.

5. Remove the pan from the oven and let cool slightly.

6. Taste and, if needed, add a pinch more salt and pepper.

7. Garnish with sliced almonds and balsamic glaze (optional), and serve hot.

*To toast almonds, place sliced almonds in a dry skillet set over medium heat. Stir the almonds frequently to make sure they do not burn. Cook the almonds for 4 to 5 minutes, or until lightly browned and toasted.

PREP TIME: 10 minutes | COOK TIME: 8-10 minutes

LITTLE ROSEMARY
HONEY BISCUITS

GREEN BEAN
ALMONDINE

RICE JARDIN

{SERVES 8}

This dish was a staple in our catering division for years. Buffets in the '80s and '90s were known for the standards: green beans, potatoes, or macaroni and cheese. The colorful presentation combined with the coriander made this a showstopper!

---

3 tablespoons salted butter

¾ cup chopped Vidalia onion

1½ pounds zucchini (4 to 5 medium zucchini), thinly sliced in half-moons

1 (15.25-ounce) can whole kernel corn, drained

1 (14.5-ounce) can diced tomatoes

3 cups cooked long grain white rice

1½ teaspoons kosher salt

1½ teaspoons freshly ground black pepper

¼ teaspoon ground coriander

¼ teaspoon dried oregano leaves

1. In a heavy-bottomed pan set over medium heat, melt the butter. Sauté the onions and zucchini in the melted butter until tender.

2. Add in the corn, diced tomatoes, rice, and seasonings. Stir to combine.

3. Cover the pan and simmer the mixture for 15 minutes, or until hot throughout.

4. Serve warm.

PREP TIME: 15-20 minutes | COOK TIME: 15-25 minutes

ROASTED BRUSSELS SPROUTS GRATIN

{MAKES 1½ QUARTS, 6 TO 9 SERVINGS}

A great way to elevate roasted Brussels sprouts is to bake them into a delicious casserole. The bacon adds just a slight smokiness to the dish that brings an added richness. For any leftovers, this recipe can also be used as a topping to a toast round for the perfect appetizer bite.

1. Preheat the oven to 400°F and prepare a 1½-quart shallow baking dish with cooking spray and set aside.

2. Place the Brussels sprouts on a large sheet pan with the olive oil, ¼ of the garlic, and salt and pepper to taste. Roast for 15 minutes.

3. Allow the roasted Brussels sprouts to cool, then roughly chop.

4. Turn the oven down to 350°F.

5. Fill a medium-large saucepan halfway with water and bring to a boil. Add in a few dashes of kosher salt.

6. Add the chopped carrots to the boiling water. Boil for 5 to 6 minutes, or until the carrots are tender. Drain the carrots and return to the saucepan. Set aside.

7. In another large skillet, cook the bacon over medium heat until crispy. Remove the bacon from the pan and set on a paper towel-lined plate to cool. Reserve the bacon drippings. When cool enough to handle, chop the bacon.

8. Add the butter, minced shallots, and remaining minced garlic to the pan with the bacon drippings. Cook over medium heat for about 1 minute, stirring constantly to make sure it does not burn. Stir in the flour to combine and remove from the heat.

9. Add the shallot mixture and chopped Brussels sprouts to the saucepan with the carrots. Stir in the chopped bacon, 1 cup Parmesan cheese, ½ teaspoon salt, and ½ teaspoon pepper. Stir to combine, then pour the vegetable mixture into the prepared casserole dish.

10. In a small mixing bowl, combine the heavy cream, mustard, and crushed red pepper flakes. Stir well and pour over the Brussels sprouts in the casserole dish.

11. In a separate bowl, combine the remaining ½ cup shredded Parmesan and the panko bread crumbs. Sprinkle evenly over the casserole.

12. Place the casserole dish in the oven and bake uncovered for 20 minutes, or until the mixture is bubbly and the topping is golden brown in color.

Cooking spray

1¼ pounds Brussels sprouts, trimmed

3 tablespoons extra-virgin olive oil

4 cloves garlic, minced, divided

Kosher salt, to taste

Freshly ground black pepper, to taste

1 cup peeled and chopped carrots

8 slices bacon

1 tablespoon unsalted butter

¼ cup minced shallots

1 tablespoon all-purpose flour

1½ cups finely grated Parmesan cheese, divided

1 cup heavy cream

1 tablespoon coarse-ground mustard

Dash crushed red pepper flakes

¼ cup panko bread crumbs

PREP TIME: 20-25 minutes | BAKE TIME: 35 minutes

CAESAR CHICKEN PASTA SALAD

{SERVES 4}

A refreshing and filling pasta salad, perfect for a warm spring day. Depending on the meal, this could be served as a side dish or as the main dish. Sweet cherry tomatoes balance the green onions, but the hand-shaved Parmesan is key!

---

1. Cook the pasta according to the package directions. Drain and let cool completely.

2. In a large bowl, toss the cooked pasta with the chicken, lettuce, tomatoes, green onions, and fresh basil.

3. Add in the salad dressing and toss to combine. Then, add in the parsley and shaved Parmesan.

4. Toss all ingredients to coat. Add more salad dressing to combine, if needed.

TIP: A rotisserie chicken is great for this recipe! Three cups is roughly one whole small rotisserie chicken shredded. If you do use a rotisserie chicken, do not use the skin.

PREP TIME: 20-25 minutes

8 ounces uncooked bowtie pasta

12 ounces (3 cups) shredded chicken breast (tip below)

2 cups thinly sliced romaine lettuce

1 cup halved cherry tomatoes

¼ cup chopped green onions

2 tablespoons thinly sliced fresh basil

⅓ cup Caesar salad dressing, plus more if needed

2 tablespoons chopped fresh parsley

4 ounces shaved Parmesan

BUTTERMILK COCONUT PIE
{MAKES 1 (9-INCH) PIE}

An Easter dessert that is perfect to share. Not overly sweet, it is the perfect way to end your big Easter dinner. Be sure to allow the pie plenty of time to cool down before serving. If you attempt to cut a pie that is still warm, you won't be able to get clean slices. I really love this pie served at room temperature.

---

1 refrigerated pie crust, unbaked

1½ cups granulated sugar

1 tablespoon all-purpose flour

½ cup (1 stick) unsalted butter, melted

3 large eggs, beaten

½ cup buttermilk, at room temperature

1 teaspoon pure vanilla extract

1 heaping cup shredded coconut

1. Preheat the oven to 350°F and place the pie crust in a 9-inch pie dish. Crimp if desired, then cover with a damp paper towel while preparing the pie mixture.

2. In a large mixing bowl, stir together the sugar, flour, melted butter, beaten eggs, buttermilk, vanilla extract, and coconut. Stir well to combine.

3. Pour the mixture into the prepared pie crust.

4. Place the pie on a sheet pan and place in the oven.

5. Bake for 60 to 70 minutes, or until firm. Check the middle by inserting a dinner knife; if it comes out clean, it is done. If the crust starts to brown too quickly, tent the pie with foil.

6. Let the pie cool completely before cutting and serving.

PREP TIME: 10-15 minutes | BAKE TIME: 60-70 minutes

BLONDIES WITH PECAN PRALINE SAUCE

{MAKES 48 (2-INCH) SQUARES}

A great alternative to a brownie that all your guests will love! The right amount of chew with a slight crunch on top. Although great by themselves, the pecan praline sauce is the perfect finishing touch. You can also serve these with a dollop of whipped cream if you are looking to go above and beyond.

―――――

1. Preheat the oven to 350°F and prepare a (13 x 18-inch) rimmed sheet pan with baking spray.

2. In a small bowl, stir together the flour, baking powder, and salt. Set aside.

3. Place the butterscotch and butter in a heat-safe glass bowl. Set over a pot of hot (not boiling) water and melt the butterscotch and butter, stirring constantly. Remove from the heat and transfer the melted mixture to a large stand mixer bowl.

4. Stir the brown sugar into the butterscotch mixture. Cool at room temperature for 5 minutes.

5. Beat the eggs and vanilla extract into the butterscotch mixture in the bowl of a stand mixer fitted with the paddle attachment. Slowly add in the flour mixture, then add the nuts. Beat until all ingredients are fully combined.

6. Spread the blondie batter into the prepared pan and bake in the oven for 20 to 25 minutes, or until the edges are golden brown and a knife inserted in the middle comes out mostly clean.

7. Remove the pan from the oven and cool completely on a wire rack. Cut into 2-inch squares.

8. To make the optional praline sauce, stir together the sweetened condensed milk and the marinade in a medium microwave-safe bowl. Heat for 2 to 3 minutes, or until heated through and slightly thickened. Stir well.

9. Spoon over the cut blondies and top with more chopped pecans, if desired.

PREP TIME: 15-20 minutes | BAKE TIME: 20-25 minutes

Baking spray

2 cups all-purpose flour

2 teaspoons baking powder

½ teaspoon kosher salt

1 (11-ounce) package butterscotch morsels

½ cup (1 stick) unsalted butter

2 cups firmly packed dark brown sugar

4 large eggs, at room temperature

1 teaspoon pure vanilla extract

1 cup chopped pecans

PRALINE SAUCE, OPTIONAL

1 (14-ounce) can sweetened condensed milk

2 tablespoons Tony Chachere's® Praline Honey Ham Injectable Marinade

¾ cup pecan halves, roughly chopped (optional)

ASPARAGUS ROLL-UPS

{SERVES 15}

A fun and different way to serve asparagus at your next gathering. This is a great recipe to call the kids into the kitchen for their help assembling. Serve the whole asparagus as a side dish, or cut each piece in half for a two-bite appetizer.

24 to 30 stalks fresh asparagus

1 loaf white bread

Hellmann's® mayonnaise, as needed

½ cup (1 stick) unsalted butter, melted

½ cup Kraft® finely grated Parmesan cheese

½ cup finely shredded Parmesan cheese

1. Snap then blanch the asparagus in boiling water set over high heat for about 5 minutes, then immediately transfer to an ice-water bath.

2. Drain the asparagus when cooled.

3. Preheat the oven to 400°F and line a sheet pan with parchment paper.

4. Trim the crust from the bread using a serrated knife. Using a rolling pin, flatten each piece of bread.

5. Spread each flattened piece with a light coating of mayonnaise.

6. Place the asparagus on the bread with some asparagus hanging over on both ends. Roll up in a jelly roll fashion.

7. Mix the two Parmesan cheeses in a shallow bowl.

8. Dip each rolled asparagus in the melted butter and then the Parmesan to coat thoroughly.

9. Place the asparagus roll-ups on the prepared sheet pan and bake for 10 to 15 minutes, or until golden brown.

NOTE: The roll-ups can be frozen and baked at a later time. To freeze, place the uncooked rolled asparagus pieces on a sheet pan with parchment paper and place the pan in the freezer. Once the roll-ups are fully frozen, store in resealable plastic bags until ready to use. Bake from a frozen state, changing the cooking time to 15 to 20 minutes.

PREP TIME: 20-35 minutes | COOK TIME: 10-15 minutes

TOMATO PIE CROSTINI

{MAKES 30 CROSTINI}

This is an adaptation from my Tomato Pie recipe in the first cookbook, *The VeryVera Cookbook: Recipes from My Table*. That recipe is a must if you have not tried it! You can use the spread on toast rounds, or in phyllo cups as a filling. Dice the tomatoes small enough that you can fit 2 to 3 small cubes on top of each crostini.

———

1. Preheat the oven to 350°F and spread out the toast rounds in a single layer on a rimmed sheet pan.

2. Mix together the cheeses, mayonnaise, green onions, and basil.

3. In a separate bowl, toss the diced Roma tomatoes with kosher salt and black pepper to taste.

4. Put ½ tablespoon of the cheese spread on top of each toast round and top with the diced tomatoes.

5. Bake in the oven for about 8 to 10 minutes, or until the spread is slightly melted.

6. Serve warm and enjoy!

PREP TIME: 20 minutes | BAKE TIME: 8-10 minutes

1 package toast rounds or phyllo cups

½ cup shredded Parmesan cheese

1 cup grated sharp cheddar cheese

¾ to 1 cup Hellmann's® mayonnaise

¼ cup sliced green onions

¼ cup freshly chopped basil

½ cup diced Roma tomatoes

Kosher salt, to taste

Freshly ground black pepper, to taste

GREEN JACKET SALAD

{ S E R V E S   6 }

The coveted Green Jacket Salad is a classic in Augusta during the biggest golf week of the year. Have all your salad ingredients ready to go before the event so you can quickly assemble the dish right before serving. Always go slowly when adding the dressing so you don't overdress and make the salad soggy. One of my favorite parts of this salad is the pita chip croutons.

DRESSING

½ cup vegetable oil

¼ cup red wine vinegar

1 teaspoon Lawry's® seasoned salt

½ teaspoon dried oregano leaves

SALAD

1 head romaine or iceberg lettuce, torn or chopped

1 large tomato, diced

2 teaspoons chopped green onion, green tops only

2 teaspoons chopped fresh parsley

2 pieces pita bread, split in half

3 tablespoons unsalted butter, melted

Kernel Season's® Butter Popcorn Seasoning, to taste

*Pita chips make a great substitution if you do not want to make your own pita croutons.

1. Preheat the oven to 200°F and line a baking sheet with parchment paper.

2. In a small mixing bowl, whisk together all dressing ingredients until well combined. Set aside until ready to use.

3. In a large bowl, mix together all salad ingredients except the pita bread, butter, and seasoning. Toss well to evenly distribute the tomato, green onion, and parsley.

4. Place the pita bread on the prepared baking sheet and brush the tops with the melted butter. Sprinkle with the butter popcorn seasoning.

5. Bake in the oven for 1 hour, or until the pita is crisp and lightly browned. Cool and break into random-sized pieces.

6. Dress the salad and top with pita croutons before serving.

PREP TIME: 15-20 minutes | BAKE TIME: 1 hour

GLAZED CRACKERS

{MAKES 60 TO 65 CRACKERS}

A foolproof sweet treat that you won't be able to stop eating. Although considered a dessert, these crackers go perfectly on a charcuterie board, especially when paired with Brie. Go ahead and make these before you cook anything else for your event, so you have something to snack on throughout the day.

Baking spray

½ cup (1 stick) margarine

½ cup (1 stick) unsalted butter

½ cup granulated sugar

1 teaspoon pure vanilla extract

1 cup chopped pecans

2 sleeves Ritz® crackers

1. Preheat the oven to 325°F and spray two rimmed sheet pans lightly with baking spray.

2. Combine the margarine, butter, and sugar in a heavy-bottomed saucepan. Stir over medium heat until it begins to boil. Boil for 3 minutes and remove from heat.

3. Add in the vanilla and pecans. Stir well.

4. Arrange the crackers on the two sheet pans in a single layer. Pour the butter mixture over the crackers to cover, brushing on the crackers as necessary and making sure the pecans are evenly distributed.

5. Bake in the oven for 8 minutes.

6. Remove from the oven and allow to cool briefly, about 5 to 7 minutes. Remove from the sheet pans with a spatula and let cool completely.

PREP TIME: 20 minutes | BAKE TIME: 8 minutes

CRAB CAKES WITH REMOULADE SAUCE AND LOW COUNTRY WAFERS

{MAKES 14 TO 16 MINI CRAB CAKES}

A perfect crab cake should obviously be heavy on the crab pieces. When mixing, be sure not to break the lump crab too small. You always want a big bite of crab! As a final touch to top the crab cake, add a dollop of my remoulade sauce. The Low Country wafers can even be enjoyed on their own!

1. In a large skillet set over medium heat, melt the butter. Add the celery and onions, and sauté until transparent. Set aside.

2. In a mixing bowl add the crab meat, half of the bread crumbs, the egg, cooked onions and celery, mayonnaise, parsley, dill, and creole seasoning. Mix gently.

3. Place the remaining bread crumbs in a pie dish.

4. Form balls of the crab mixture (about 1 ounce or the size of a quarter), and flatten each to ¼-inch thick. Coat each crab cake in the remaining bread crumbs.

5. Sauté crab cakes in a large skillet with olive oil set over medium-high heat. Cook approximately 2 minutes per side, or until golden brown.

6. For the wafers, preheat the oven to 275°F and line a sheet pan with foil. Place a wire cooling rack in the prepared pan.

7. Melt the butter in a saucepan.

8. Dip the saltines in the melted butter and place on the prepared rack. Place in the oven and bake for 30 minutes.

9. Let cool before serving. Crackers can be stored in an airtight container at room temperature.

10. For the remoulade sauce, combine all ingredients thoroughly in a mixing bowl, adjusting creole seasoning to taste.

11. Chill until ready to serve.

12. Assemble the cooked crab cakes on top of the wafers. Dollop with the remoulade sauce and enjoy!

NOTE: The remoulade sauce will keep in an airtight container in the refrigerator for up to two weeks, so feel free to make the sauce in advance.

PREP TIME: 55 minutes | COOK TIME: 40-50 minutes

CRAB CAKES

1 tablespoon unsalted butter

½ cup diced celery

½ cup diced Vidalia onion

1 pound lump crab meat

½ cup dry plain bread crumbs, divided

1 large egg, beaten

3 tablespoons Hellmann's® mayonnaise

1 teaspoon minced fresh parsley

1 teaspoon minced fresh dill

1 teaspoon Tony Chachere's® Creole Seasoning

Extra-virgin olive oil, as needed for cooking

LOW COUNTRY WAFERS

½ cup (1 stick) salted butter

1 sleeve saltine crackers

REMOULADE SAUCE

1 cup mayonnaise

1 tablespoon freshly squeezed lemon juice

1 tablespoon dill pickle relish

1 tablespoon capers, chopped

1 garlic clove, minced

2 teaspoons Dijon-style mustard

1 teaspoon finely chopped flat-leaf parsley

½ to 1 teaspoon Tabasco® hot sauce, depending on preference

½ teaspoon Worcestershire sauce

⅛ teaspoon dried tarragon

1 to 2 teaspoons Tony Chachere's® Creole Seasoning

THE VELVET HAMMER
{SERVES 6 TO 8}

An adult milkshake! This is a beloved drink in Augusta and it comes together very quickly. Your guests will love this sweet treat to end the night.

1. Place all ingredients in a blender.

2. Blend until smooth and combined. This drink is very much based on your own preferences, so feel free to adjust the amounts of alcohol to your taste.

3. Pour the milkshake into glasses and top with whipped cream and a cherry on top.

4. Enjoy responsibly!

PREP TIME: 5 minutes

1 (1½-quart) container Breyer's vanilla ice cream, slightly softened

½ cup vodka, or adjusted to taste

⅓ cup Kahlúa® Coffee Liqueur, or adjusted to taste

Whipped cream, for topping

Maraschino cherries, for garnish

MACAROON PIE
{MAKES 1 (9-INCH) PIE}

Save this recipe as one of the easiest desserts to prepare. The saltines are perfectly balanced by the sweet dates. This dessert is both crunchy and chewy, and extremely light! A great dessert to end a heavy meal.

1. Preheat the oven to 350°F and prepare a pie dish with baking spray.

2. Whip the egg whites in the bowl of a stand mixer fitted with the whisk attachment until medium peaks form. Slowly add in the sugar, continuing to beat, until you have stiff peaks.

3. In a separate mixing bowl, mix together the saltine crumbs, chopped dates, chopped pecans, almond extract, and baking powder.

4. Fold in the whipped egg whites until the mixture is just incorporated.

5. Gently pour the mixture into the prepared pie dish.

6. Bake for 30 to 35 minutes, or until the mixture is lightly golden.

7. Remove from the oven and let cool completely in the pie dish.

8. Slice and serve topped with whipped cream.

Baking spray

3 large egg whites

1 cup granulated sugar

12 saltines, crumbled

12 pitted dates, chopped

1 cup pecans, roughly chopped

¼ teaspoon almond extract

¼ teaspoon baking powder

Whipped cream, for topping

PREP TIME: 20 minutes | BAKE TIME: 30-35 minutes

Pictured on page 31

PEANUT BUTTER PIE

{MAKES 1 (9-INCH) PIE}

Everybody who knows me knows how much I love peanut butter. So obviously there is no doubt that this is one of my favorite desserts! The recipe below uses an oatmeal crust, but you could also choose to use a chocolate cookie crust. Have fun with the toppings on the pie and add as much extra chocolate drizzle or peanuts as you want!

OATMEAL CRUST

2 cups rolled oats

½ cup sliced almonds

½ cup (1 stick) margarine, at room temperature

¼ cup firmly packed light brown sugar

FILLING

8 ounces cream cheese, at room temperature

2 cups confectioners' sugar

1 (8-ounce) container Cool Whip®

12 ounces (1 ⅓ cups) Jif® creamy peanut butter

2 teaspoons pure vanilla extract

MARSHMALLOW MERINGUE

3 large egg whites, at room temperature

3 tablespoons granulated sugar, divided

1 cup marshmallow creme

Chopped lightly salted peanuts, as garnish

Hot caramel or chocolate sauce, as garnish

1. Preheat the oven to 375°F. In a large bowl, combine the ingredients for the oatmeal crust until well mixed. Using your hands, press the mixture into an oven-proof glass 9-inch pie dish, forming an even pie crust around the sides and on the bottom. Bake for 10 minutes and remove from the oven to cool.

2. In the bowl of a stand mixer, whip the cream cheese for 10 minutes with the whisk attachment.

3. Add in confectioners' sugar and whip for another 10 minutes.

4. By hand, fold in the whipped topping, peanut butter, and vanilla extract. Spread into the prepared pie crust and freeze for at least 2 hours.

5. When you're almost ready to serve the pie, make the marshmallow meringue. In a large bowl, beat the egg whites with an electric mixer until they hold soft peaks. Gradually add the granulated sugar, 1 tablespoon at a time, beating well after each addition. When the whites are thick and glossy, but not dry, add the marshmallow creme and blend on low speed. Fold with a spatula if necessary.

6. Using a rubber spatula, spread the meringue evenly over the pie, mounding it slightly in the center. Place pie in the freezer for about 5 minutes.

7. Just before serving, preheat the broiler. Set the pie on a baking sheet and place under the broiler, removing when meringue is golden brown. Don't leave the oven, the meringue will take a very short time to brown.

8. Add chopped peanuts and drizzle the caramel or chocolate sauce over the top.

9. Serve immediately and store any leftovers in the freezer for up to 5 days. Remove from the freezer to let soften slightly before eating leftovers.

PREP TIME: 45 minutes | BAKE/FREEZE TIME: 2 hours and 5 minutes

SEA ISLAND SHRIMP

{MAKES 12 TO 14 APPETIZER-SIZED SERVINGS}

In the '80s and early '90s, ice sculptures were the "ultimate" display vessels at wedding receptions. One of our favorite appetizers to serve from an ice seashell, this dish was always a guest favorite.

———

1. In a medium bowl, add the olive oil, canola oil, vinegar, capers, sugar, hot sauce, and salt. Whisk until well combined.

2. In a large storage bowl, combine the shrimp, onion, tomatoes, and black olives. Mix in the marinade and combine thoroughly.

3. Place the lemon slices on top of shrimp mixture and cover the bowl with its lid, if possible, or with plastic wrap.

4. Refrigerate for at least 12 hours, or until the shrimp has marinated and all the flavors have combined.

5. Serve drained over lettuce leaves with toothpicks.

TIP: To cook shrimp, bring 4 quarts of water to a boil. Add in ⅓ cup Old Bay® Seasoning and let boil for about 1 minute. Add shrimp in the shell and stir. Turn off the heat and put the lid on the pot. Let shrimp sit in the hot water for 1 to 2 minutes, or until pink. Pour out into a colander and cover with ice.

PREP TIME: 15-20 minutes | CHILL TIME: 12 hours

½ cup extra-virgin olive oil

½ cup canola oil

¾ cup apple cider vinegar

1 (3.5-ounce) container capers, with juice

⅓ cup granulated sugar

2 tablespoons Tabasco® hot sauce

½ teaspoon kosher salt

2 ½ pounds jumbo (21/25) shrimp, cooked and peeled

1 ½ medium Vidalia onions, cut in small wedges

2 large tomatoes, cored and cubed into bite-sized pieces

1 cup whole black olives, pitted

1 to 2 lemons, sliced

Lettuce leaves, for serving

SWEET LITTLE BLTs WITH MAPLE-CANDIED BACON

{MAKES 30 BITES}

During the golf tournament in Augusta, 19th hole celebrations take place all over our city. This is one of our clients' favorites and has become a staple on our menus. This recipe goes great on a table with Egg Salad and Pimento Cheese sandwiches. Both of those classic recipes can be found in my first cookbook, *The VeryVera Cookbook: Recipes from My Table.*

BLTs

6 slices center-cut bacon

8 ounces cream cheese, at room temperature

2 tablespoons Hellmann's® mayonnaise

¾ teaspoon garlic powder

1 tablespoon diced green onions

10 slices white sandwich bread

½ cup cherry tomatoes, sliced into thirds for garnish

1 cup Maple-Candied Bacon (see below)

MAPLE-CANDIED BACON

2 tablespoons pure maple syrup

¼ cup firmly packed light brown sugar

1½ teaspoons bourbon, optional

1½ teaspoons Dijon-style mustard

½ pound center-cut bacon

1. Preheat the oven to 350°F.

2. Cook the slices of bacon on the stove and drain on paper towels. When cool enough to handle, crumble and set aside.

3. In a bowl of a stand mixer, beat the cream cheese and mayonnaise with the paddle attachment until smooth.

4. Add the garlic powder and the crumbled bacon to the cream cheese mixture and mix well. Fold in the green onions and set aside.

5. Using a round cutter, cut pieces of the white bread into 1-inch circles. Place the bread circles on a sheet pan and toast in the oven for 5 minutes, watching carefully to ensure a light golden brown.

6. Remove from the oven and allow the toast rounds to cool.

7. Spread about ¼-inch of the dip on top of each toast round.

8. Place a small slice of cherry tomato and a piece of the maple-candied bacon (recipe follows) on top of the dip.

9. For the maple-candied bacon, preheat the oven to 350°F and prepare a sheet pan with foil and a baking rack.

10. In a medium bowl, mix together the maple syrup, brown sugar, bourbon (if desired), and mustard. Stir until thoroughly combined.

11. Dip the bacon pieces in the mixture, thoroughly coating the bacon.

12. Place bacon on the rack on the baking sheet and bake for 15 minutes.

13. Remove the pan from the oven and flip the bacon. Bake for an additional 10 minutes, or until it starts to stiffen.

14. Remove from oven and cool slightly before cutting into small pieces.

15. Use any leftover bacon for a snack or as a delicious garnish in a Bloody Mary!

PREP TIME: 25 minutes | COOK TIME: 30-35 minutes

THE AZALEA

{MAKES 1 DRINK}

The classic golf cocktail that is both beautiful and delicious! This drink is named after the flowers that are in bloom in Augusta during the golf tournament every spring. Garnish each drink with a lemon wedge and green striped straw.

1. Pour the gin, pineapple juice, lemon juice, and grenadine in a cocktail shaker with ice. Shake vigorously for 1 minute.

2. Strain the contents of the shaker into a tall cocktail or coupe glass filled with ice.

3. Garnish with a lemon wedge and enjoy!

PREP TIME: 5 minutes

1 ½ ounces gin (or vodka can be substituted if you prefer)

2 ounces fresh pineapple juice

1 ounce freshly squeezed lemon juice

1 teaspoon grenadine

Lemon wedge, to garnish

CHEESE CRISPIES

{MAKES 60 WAFERS}

This is one of the original recipes I remember of my mother-in-law, Sue Stewart, and I still think about her when I make them! She always said to finely grate the cheese, which is very important in preparing these crackers.

1. Preheat the oven to 325°F.

2. In a large mixing bowl, combine the grated cheese and margarine. Mix well by hand.

3. Add in the flour, red pepper, and Rice Krispies®. Mix well. This is easiest using your hands until the mixture comes together.

4. Form into balls, about the size of a marble.

5. Place on an ungreased cookie sheet and press with a fork dipped in water to flatten twice, alternating directions, flattening each crisp until about ⅛-inch thick. Dip the fork in water between pressing each ball.

6. Bake for 18 to 20 minutes, until lightly browned and crispy.

PREP TIME: 15 minutes | BAKE TIME: 18-20 minutes

1 (8-ounce) package Cracker Barrel® sharp cheddar cheese, finely grated with Zyliss® rotary cheese grater

½ cup (1 stick) Land O Lakes® margarine, at room temperature

1 cup all-purpose flour

⅛ teaspoon ground red pepper

1 cup Rice Krispies® cereal

BETTY'S BANANA NUT POUND CAKE

{MAKES 1 CAKE, 24 SERVINGS}

An upgrade from banana bread that can be served as dessert or maybe even breakfast. Warm a slice of this dense cake and put a smear of peanut butter on top. A delicious combination that even Elvis would approve!

POUND CAKE

Baking spray

1 cup (2 sticks) unsalted butter, at room temperature

3 cups granulated sugar

1 cup heavy cream

1 teaspoon pure vanilla extract

3 cups cake flour

½ teaspoon ground cinnamon

½ teaspoon ground nutmeg

¼ teaspoon ground cloves

½ teaspoon kosher salt

6 large eggs, at room temperature

3 ripe bananas, chopped

½ cup pecans, chopped

⅓ cup toasted coconut chips, to garnish

1 cup Banana Icing

BANANA ICING

1 cup Cream Cheese Icing (*The VeryVera Cookbook: Recipes from my Table*, page 100)

½ teaspoon banana flavoring

1. Preheat the oven to 325°F and prepare a large 12-cup Bundt pan with baking spray.

2. In the mixing bowl of a stand mixer fitted with the paddle attachment, cream the butter and sugar on medium speed for 20 minutes, or until light and fluffy.

3. While the butter and sugar are mixing, measure out the remaining ingredients for the pound cake. In a liquid measuring cup, whisk together the cream and vanilla extract. In another bowl, whisk together the cake flour, cinnamon, nutmeg, cloves, and salt.

4. Once the butter and sugar have finished creaming, scrape the sides and bottom of the bowl. With the mixer on low speed, add the eggs one at a time, beating well after each addition. Scrape the sides and bottom of the bowl again, then add in the chopped bananas and beat on medium speed for about 1 minute. Turn the mixer down to low speed and beat for 5 minutes.

5. With the mixer still on low speed, alternately add the flour mixture and the cream mixture, beginning and ending with the flour mixture. Mix until well combined. Scrape the sides of the bowl and incorporate any unmixed batter if necessary.

6. Add in the pecans. Mix on low speed until well blended but do not over-mix. Pour the batter into the prepared Bundt pan until it is about 1 to 1 ½ inches from the top. Tap the pan on the counter to ensure there are no air bubbles. (If there is remaining batter, use it to make muffins.)

7. Bake for 1 hour and 20 minutes. To test doneness, insert a wooden skewer into the cake; if the skewer comes out clean, the cake is ready.

8. If your icing is cold, allow it to come to room temperature before mixing in the banana flavoring. If freshly prepared, immediately add the flavoring to the icing. Taste to be sure there is a banana flavor. If not, add another ¼ teaspoon banana flavoring.

9. Prepare a piping bag with your choice of tip. Scoop the icing into the piping bag. Decorate by piping the top and sides of the cake.

PREP TIME: 30-35 minutes | BAKE TIME: 1 hour and 20 minutes

BLUE CHEESE WAFERS

{MAKES 100 WAFERS}

These blue cheese wafers make a great snack for cocktail hour or serve them on the side of the classic wedge or any other salad. Top with fig preserves or bacon jam as a passed appetizer. The wafers can be stored in an airtight container for up to one week.

---

1. In the bowl of a food processor, mix the blue cheese, butter, and flour all at once. Scrape down the bowl as needed; the mixture should be sticky. Remove and place in a larger mixing bowl.

2. Add in the pecans and mix well.

3. Cover the bowl and chill for 30 minutes.

4. Roll the dough into 10-inch logs, 1 to 2 inches in diameter. Wrap the individual logs and chill for 1 hour, but preferably overnight.

5. When ready to bake, preheat the oven to 350°F and line sheet pans with parchment paper.

6. Slice the chilled dough into ¼-inch-thick round wafers, about the size of a cracker.

7. Place on the prepared baking sheet pan and bake for 17 minutes, or until golden brown.

PREP TIME: 10 minutes | CHILL TIME: 1 hour and 30 minutes
BAKE TIME: 17 minutes

8 ounces blue cheese, softened

1 cup (2 sticks) unsalted butter, at room temperature

2 ½ cups all-purpose flour

¾ cup chopped pecans

LEMON CHICKEN PARMESAN

{SERVES 6}

I've put my "twist" on the classic chicken Parmesan. The lemon addition makes this slightly lighter than the original. You can serve it with pasta on the side. If you choose to add pasta, I would stick to a light sauce of olive oil, garlic, and some Parmesan cheese.

CHICKEN PARMESAN

1 cup all-purpose flour

Kosher salt

Freshly ground black pepper

2 large eggs

1 tablespoon water

1½ cups panko bread crumbs

½ cup freshly grated Parmesan cheese

1½ teaspoons lemon zest

1 teaspoon fresh thyme leaves, chopped

6 boneless, skinless chicken breasts

Szeged® Chicken Rub, as needed

2 tablespoons unsalted butter, divided

2 tablespoons extra-virgin olive oil, divided

¼ pound Parmesan wedge, shaved

Radishes, thinly sliced, to garnish (optional)

ARUGULA SALAD

½ cup freshly squeezed lemon juice

1 cup extra-virgin olive oil

1 teaspoon kosher salt

½ teaspoon freshly ground black pepper

10 ounces arugula, washed

1. In a glass pie pan or shallow bowl, add the flour and season lightly with salt and pepper.

2. In a second pie pan or bowl, beat the eggs and add the water.

3. Finally, in a third pan or bowl, mix together the panko bread crumbs, grated Parmesan cheese, lemon zest, and chopped thyme.

4. Using a meat mallet, pound each chicken breast between two sheets of parchment paper until they are about ½-inch thick. Season each piece of chicken lightly with the Szeged® Chicken Rub.

5. Coat both sides of each chicken breast in the flour, then in the egg mixture, and finally in the breadcrumb mixture, pressing to coat.

6. In a large sauté pan set over medium heat, add 1 tablespoon unsalted butter and 1 tablespoon olive oil.

7. Cook the chicken breasts in the pan for about 3 to 4 minutes per side, or until a thermometer inserted in the middle of the thickest part of the chicken reads 165°F.

8. Continue to cook the remaining chicken breasts, adding more butter and olive oil as needed.

9. While the chicken is cooking, prepare the arugula salad.

10. In a small mixing bowl, combine the lemon juice, olive oil, salt, and pepper. Whisk to combine.

11. Pour the dressing on the arugula, as much as desired, and toss well.

12. Place the dressed arugula on a serving plate and top with the whole or sliced chicken breasts. Add shaved Parmesan and thinly sliced radishes as desired.

PREP TIME: 20 minutes | COOK TIME: 15 minutes

GARDEN SPAGHETTI SALAD
{*MAKES 10 TO 12 SERVINGS*}

A fun twist on the classic pasta salad, this dish can be served cold or at room temperature. This is a delicious spring side using classic Southern ingredients. This salad is great with in-season produce but do not fret, this salad is just as delicious with frozen vegetables.

SPAGHETTI

8 ounces dry spaghetti, broken into 2-inch pieces

1 tablespoon extra-virgin olive oil or vegetable oil

2 cups cooked corn

2 cups cooked lima beans

1 ½ cups halved cherry tomatoes

½ cup thinly sliced green onions

⅓ cup minced fresh parsley

6 bacon strips, cooked and crumbled

DRESSING

⅓ cup extra-virgin olive oil

3 tablespoons red wine vinegar

2 tablespoons freshly squeezed lemon juice

1 teaspoon granulated sugar

1 teaspoon kosher salt

¼ teaspoon paprika

Freshly ground black pepper, to taste

1. Cook the spaghetti according to the package directions; drain and rinse in cold water.

2. Place cooked spaghetti in a large bowl and toss with 1 tablespoon of extra-virgin olive oil or vegetable oil.

3. Add in the corn, lima beans, tomatoes, green onions, parsley, and bacon. Toss to mix well.

4. In a cruet or lidded jar, combine the extra-virgin olive oil with the vinegar. Add in the lemon juice, sugar, and seasonings. Shake until the mixture comes together.

5. Pour the dressing over the spaghetti mixture; toss gently.

6. Serve immediately. If you plan on serving later, mix the salad ingredients and toss with the dressing right before serving.

PREP TIME: 45 minutes

Pictured on page 65

ASPARAGUS CASSEROLE
{MAKES 1 (2½-QUART) CASSEROLE DISH}

Look no further for a different way to serve asparagus to family and friends. This comforting casserole is not too heavy and has been updated to substitute fresh mushrooms instead of the classic canned mushrooms. The mix of the fried onion pieces and crushed Ritz® crackers makes a buttery and crunchy topping that will be hard to resist.

1. Preheat the oven to 350°F and prepare a 2 ½-quart casserole dish with cooking spray.

2. Lay the chopped asparagus on the bottom of the casserole dish.

3. In a saucepan set over medium-low heat, stir 6 tablespoons of the unsalted butter until melted. Slowly stir in the flour until it has combined and created a roux. It will be blonde in color and thick.

4. While stirring constantly, slowly pour in the milk. Continue to stir and pour until all the milk has been incorporated. Turn heat to low and continue to stir until the sauce has thickened. Season with salt and pepper.

5. Remove the white sauce from heat and pour over the asparagus.

6. Sprinkle the cheese over the asparagus and white sauce and set the casserole dish to the side.

7. In a medium sauté pan, heat 1 tablespoon unsalted butter and cook the mushroom slices until they have softened and most of the liquid has cooked out. Season with salt and pepper to taste. Remove from heat.

8. Add the mushrooms and any liquid from the pan to the casserole dish and top with the fried onions.

9. In a microwave-safe bowl, melt the remaining 2 tablespoons unsalted butter.

10. In a separate small bowl, crush the Ritz® crackers and stir in the melted butter. Once combined, sprinkle over the top of the casserole.

11. Bake for 30 to 35 minutes, or until heated through. Serve hot.

PREP TIME: 35 minutes | BAKE TIME: 30-35 minutes

Cooking spray

2 bunches asparagus, trimmed and chopped into 1-inch pieces

9 tablespoons unsalted butter, divided

6 tablespoons all-purpose flour

2 cups whole milk

Kosher salt, to taste

Freshly ground black pepper, to taste

1 cup freshly shredded sharp cheddar cheese

2 cups sliced fresh mushrooms

1 (2.8-ounce) container French's® crispy fried onions

15 Ritz® crackers

SPINACH AND FETA STUFFED CHICKEN BREASTS

{SERVES 4 TO 5}

A delicious way to elevate the average chicken breast! A delicious stuffing and perfect lemon caper sauce on top will make your guests think you were in the kitchen for hours. For a beautiful presentation, slice the chicken breasts and fan out the slices before serving so your guests are intrigued by the stuffing.

SPINACH AND CHEESE STUFFING

Cooking spray

1 tablespoon unsalted butter

1 Vidalia onion, chopped

12 ounces fresh spinach, washed, stemmed, and coarsely chopped

½ cup crumbled feta cheese

½ cup drained sun-dried tomatoes

Kosher salt, to taste

Freshly ground black pepper, to taste

4 to 5 frozen boneless, skinless chicken breasts, thawed

Extra-virgin olive oil, as needed

1 teaspoon fresh thyme (or ¼ teaspoon dried thyme)

½ teaspoon kosher salt

LEMON CAPER SAUCE

4 tablespoons unsalted butter

3 tablespoons flour

1 tablespoon Better Than Bouillon® Roasted Chicken Base

¾ cup hot water

1 ½ cups half-and-half

3 tablespoons capers

2 tablespoons freshly squeezed lemon juice

Kosher salt, to taste

Freshly ground black pepper, to taste

1. Preheat the oven to 375°F and prepare a 9 x 13-inch baking dish with cooking spray.

2. To prepare the stuffing, melt butter in a large saucepan set over medium heat. Cook the onion in melted butter until the onion is translucent.

3. Add the spinach to the pan and cook until it is wilted and the moisture has evaporated, about 3 to 5 minutes. Transfer the mixture to a bowl and cool.

4. Stir the feta cheese and sun-dried tomatoes into the onion and spinach. Season with salt and pepper. Set stuffing aside.

5. Pound the chicken breasts thinly. Spoon the stuffing on the inside of each chicken breast. Fold over the breast and secure with toothpicks.

6. Brush the chicken with olive oil and sprinkle each chicken breast with thyme and salt.

7. Bake for 45 to 50 minutes, or until a thermometer inserted into the thickest part of the chicken breast reads 165°F.

8. While the chicken is baking, prepare the lemon caper sauce.

9. In a medium saucepan over medium-low heat, melt the butter. Once the butter has melted, stir in the flour. Stir with a wooden spoon to combine.

10. In a separate mixing bowl, whisk the chicken base with the hot water to create chicken broth.

11. While stirring, slowly pour the chicken broth into the flour and butter mixture. Continue to stir until it is combined and very thick.

12. Pour in the half-and-half while still stirring. The mixture will start to thin, but once all the liquid has been added, the sauce will begin to thicken again and should coat the back of the spoon.

13. Remove the sauce from heat and add in the capers and lemon juice. Season with salt and pepper.

14. When ready to serve, pour the lemon caper sauce over the top of the chicken and enjoy!

PREP TIME: 35 minutes | COOK TIME: 45-50 minutes

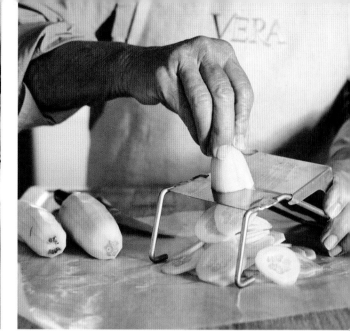

SUE'S CUCUMBER SALAD

{SERVES 10}

This is easily one of my top five recipes. I remember so vividly watching my mother-in-law, Sue Stewart, make this recipe. Of course, she gathered the cucumbers from Aunt Tut's garden, making the process even more special. It has been my goal that this recipe and the technique behind it stand the test of time. The key is to salt, rinse, and squeeze the excess water out of the cucumbers so they stay nice and crisp in the salad.

---

1. Place the sliced cucumbers in a bowl in a single layer. Sprinkle with salt and repeat with a second salted layer until all cucumbers have been used. Refrigerate for at least 6 hours, or overnight.

2. Drain and rinse the sliced and salted cucumbers. Squeeze by hand to get excess water out, then put 3 handfuls at a time in a long row in the center of a tea towel. Roll the towel up and twist the towel to get the remaining water out and then transfer to a large mixing bowl.

3. Add in the sour cream, mayonnaise, and sliced green onions, and gently mix.

4. Season with black pepper to taste and try the mixture before adding more salt.

5. Chill. This salad will last in the refrigerator for 3 to 4 days.

6 to 8 pickling cucumbers, peeled and cut ⅛-inch thick with a mandoline slicer

1 teaspoon kosher salt, plus more for seasoning

¼ cup sour cream

⅓ cup Hellmann's® mayonnaise

2 green onions, using both green and white parts, thinly sliced

Freshly ground black pepper, to taste

PREP TIME: 20 minutes | CHILL TIME: 6 hours or more

SOPHISTICATED HAM SANDWICH

{MAKES 5 SANDWICHES}

The name says it all…not your typical ham sandwich but definitely your new favorite. This was a customer favorite at the Café and it has not gone out of style. A great sandwich to make for a crowd. You can use a large ciabatta loaf that has been sliced but I definitely prefer the small individual loaves for this sandwich.

———

PRALINE SAUCE

½ cup (1 stick) unsalted butter

¾ cup firmly packed light brown sugar

½ cup light Karo® corn syrup

SANDWICHES

Individual ciabatta loaves, sliced in half

Praline Sauce (about ⅔ cup)

2 to 3 Granny Smith apples, thinly sliced

1 pound deli ham, thinly sliced

¼ pound Swiss cheese, thinly sliced

1. Preheat the oven to 350°F and line a sheet pan with aluminum foil or parchment paper.

2. In a medium saucepan set over medium heat, melt the butter. Once the butter has melted, add in the sugar and stir constantly until sugar has dissolved.

3. Add the corn syrup to the saucepan and stir to combine. Turn the heat off once the mixture has fully incorporated. Set aside until ready to assemble the sandwiches.

4. Lay out the sliced individual ciabatta loaves to cover the entire cookie sheet, cut-side up.

5. Spread 2 tablespoons of the praline sauce over each piece of ciabatta.

6. Layer 2 to 3 thin slices of Granny Smith apple over the bottom-half pieces of the loaves, then add 3 to 4 slices of ham and 1 slice of Swiss cheese per sandwich. Leave the sandwiches open-faced in the oven while baking to caramelize the praline sauce and melt the cheese.

7. Place the pan in the oven and bake for 8 to 10 minutes, or until the cheese has completely melted.

8. Serve warm and enjoy!

NOTE: The praline sauce can be prepared, refrigerated, and saved for another time. This is great if you are only wanting to prepare a few sandwiches at a time.

PREP TIME: 10 minutes | COOK TIME: 8-10 minutes

SPAGHETTI SAUCE

1½ pounds ground beef (80/20)

1 tablespoon extra-virgin olive oil

12 ounces sliced portobello mushrooms

1½ cups diced Vidalia onion

½ cup diced bell pepper (red or green)

2 garlic cloves, minced

2 (15-ounce) cans tomato sauce

2 (14.5-ounce) cans diced tomatoes with basil, garlic, and oregano

1 (6-ounce) can tomato paste

½ cup water

¼ cup red wine

2 teaspoons granulated sugar

¼ cup chopped flat leaf parsley

¼ teaspoon dried rosemary

¼ teaspoon dried thyme

½ teaspoon dried oregano

½ teaspoon dried basil

½ teaspoon kosher salt

½ teaspoon freshly ground black pepper

2 bay leaves

1 to 2 (16-ounce) boxes vermicelli noodles, for serving

MEATBALLS

1 pound ground beef (80/20)

¾ pound ground Italian sausage: mild

½ cup Italian bread crumbs

½ cup diced Vidalia onion

¼ cup chopped flat leaf parsley

1 garlic clove, minced

1 teaspoon kosher salt

½ teaspoon freshly ground black pepper

1 tablespoon Worcestershire sauce

1 large egg, beaten

¼ cup whole milk

2 tablespoons extra-virgin olive oil (plus more as needed)

BITSY'S SPAGHETTI SAUCE WITH MEATBALLS
{SERVES 10 TO 12}

Let this sauce simmer all day and fill your house with its delicious aroma. It is such a classic sauce—the entire family will love it. Serve with spaghetti or your choice of pasta.

SPAGHETTI SAUCE

1. In a Dutch oven, cook and crumble the ground beef over medium heat until browned.

2. Remove the cooked beef from the pan and set aside on a plate with a paper towel.

3. Add 1 tablespoon of olive oil to the pan over medium heat. Add in the sliced mushrooms, diced onion, diced bell pepper, and garlic.

4. Sauté the vegetables until soft and the onions are translucent.

5. Add in the remaining ingredients, except for pasta, and stir to combine. Once combined, stir in the ground beef.

6. Bring the mixture to a simmer and reduce the heat to low. Cover the Dutch oven and cook the spaghetti sauce over low heat throughout the day, at least 4 hours.

7. If preferred, the spaghetti sauce can be transferred to a slow cooker on low.

8. Store any leftovers in the refrigerator or freeze the leftover spaghetti sauce for later use.

MEATBALLS

1. Preheat the oven to 350°F and prepare a rimmed sheet pan with cooking spray.

2. In a large bowl, stir together the ground beef, Italian sausage, bread crumbs, onion, parsley, garlic, salt, and pepper until combined.

3. Add in the Worcestershire, beaten egg, and milk. Stir until all the ingredients come together.

4. Gently shape into 1½- to 2-inch balls.

5. In a large skillet, heat olive oil over medium heat. Add in the meatballs and brown on all sides, about 2 to 3 minutes. Continue until all the meatballs are browned, adding more olive oil as needed.

6. Transfer the browned meatballs onto the sheet pan and place pan in the oven.

7. Bake for 20 minutes, or until a thermometer inserted in the center of the meatballs reads 165°F.

8. Remove from the oven and serve with the spaghetti sauce.

PREP TIME: 60 minutes | COOK TIME: 4-6 hours

CHEESY ARTICHOKE TOAST

{MAKES 16 TOAST STRIPS}

A perfect toast to serve with a salad, spaghetti and meatballs, or lasagna—
or it makes a great appetizer. This is an easy recipe to increase if needed,
depending on the size of your party.

———

1. Preheat broiler. Broil bread slices until crisp, directly on rack,
   1 to 2 minutes per side. Transfer to a baking sheet and reduce
   oven temperature to 425°F.

2. In a medium bowl, combine artichokes, garlic, Parmesan,
   Gruyère, sour cream, lemon zest, salt, and pepper.

3. Spoon artichoke mixture on the toast slices and sprinkle
   with panko.

4. Bake until golden brown and cheese is melted, 8 to 10 minutes.
   Sprinkle with chopped parsley, if desired.

PREP TIME: 10-15 minutes | COOK TIME: 10-15 minutes

4 thick slices sourdough bread, each cut into 4 strips

1 (14-ounce) can artichoke hearts, drained and roughly chopped

1 garlic clove, finely minced

2 ounces Parmesan cheese, grated (about ¾ cup)

1 ounce Gruyère cheese, coarsely grated (about ½ cup)

2 tablespoons sour cream

½ teaspoon finely grated lemon zest

¼ teaspoon kosher salt

¼ teaspoon freshly ground black pepper

2 tablespoons panko bread crumbs

¼ cup fresh flat-leaf parsley, chopped

POPPY SEED DRESSING
{MAKES 2 CUPS}

½ cup granulated sugar

1 teaspoon kosher salt

½ cup white vinegar

1 cup vegetable oil

1 heaping tablespoon poppy seeds

A classic dressing that you can mix together and keep in the refrigerator. This slightly sweet dressing is perfect for a salad with spring mix, strawberries, and candied almonds or to dress up a bowl of fresh fruit.

1. In a blender, pour in the sugar, salt, and white vinegar. Blend until combined.

2. With the blender running, slowly pour in the vegetable oil. Continue to blend until fully combined.

3. Add in the poppy seeds and blend until incorporated.

4. Store in the refrigerator until ready to use. As the dressing sits, it will separate; whisk to recombine before serving.

PREP TIME: 5 minutes

Pictured on page 103

MANDARIN TOSSED SALAD

{SERVES 4 TO 6}

This refreshing salad is sure to become a family favorite with everybody. The sweet, candied almonds and mandarin oranges are balanced by the slightly tart red wine vinaigrette. Go ahead and candy the almonds ahead of time to cut down on the prep time for the salad. Just be sure to not snack on too many before it's time to toss the salad!

---

1. Place ¼ cup granulated sugar in a small heavy-bottomed pan set over low heat. Stir constantly until the sugar is dissolved and turns golden in color, about 8 to 10 minutes. Add in the almonds to the caramelized sugar and stir to combine.

2. Remove the candied almonds to a piece of parchment paper and spread flat as best as possible. Let cool and harden before breaking into bite-sized pieces.

3. Assemble the salad by tossing the lettuce, oranges, celery, and scallions together in a large mixing bowl.

4. In a cruet or lidded jar, combine the vegetable oil, red wine vinegar, sugar, kosher salt, and black pepper. Shake until combined.

5. Toss the salad with the dressing and top with the candied almonds.

PREP TIME: 25 minutes

Pictured on page 65

CANDIED ALMONDS

¼ cup granulated sugar

¼ cup slivered almonds

SALAD

1 head iceberg lettuce, chopped for salad

1 (11-ounce) can mandarin oranges, drained

1 cup chopped celery

2 scallions, chopped

¼ cup vegetable oil

2 tablespoons red wine vinegar

2 tablespoons granulated sugar

½ teaspoon kosher salt

Dash freshly ground black pepper

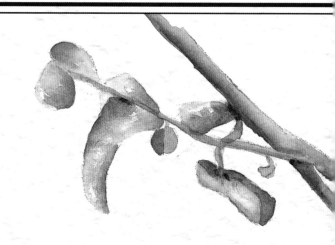

CHAPTER 2

Summer Celebrations

CAJUN SHRIMP

{SERVES 6 TO 8}

An easy sheet pan protein that you can easily pair with grits, rice, or your favorite pasta. Once the shrimp come out of the oven, try to avoid the urge to quickly pop a few in your mouth before serving! Top with fresh lemon slices for the final garnish.

Cooking spray

¼ cup extra-virgin olive oil

¼ cup Worcestershire sauce

1 teaspoon kosher salt

2 teaspoons freshly ground black pepper

1 teaspoon minced garlic

2 teaspoons dried oregano

½ teaspoon cayenne pepper

½ teaspoon Tabasco® hot sauce

2 pounds extra-large shrimp (26/30 count), peeled and deveined

2 lemons, sliced

6 tablespoons unsalted butter, cut into small pieces

1. Preheat the oven to 350°F and prepare a sheet pan with cooking spray.

2. In a mixing bowl, combine the extra-virgin olive oil, Worcestershire, kosher salt, pepper, garlic, oregano, cayenne, and Tabasco®. Mix well.

3. Pat the shrimp dry and spread out on the prepared sheet pan.

4. Pour the olive oil mixture over all of the shrimp. Dot the shrimp with the pieces of butter and place the lemon slices on top.

5. Bake for 5 to 7 minutes or until the shrimp turn pink. Halfway through, give the shrimp a stir in the pan.

6. Serve with the Herb Tomato Salad, page 76, and grits or risotto.

PREP TIME: 15-20 minutes | COOK TIME: 5-7 minutes

CHOCOLATE DELIGHT

{MAKES 1 (9 X 13-INCH) PAN, SERVES 12}

This recipe was the hottest thing going on in the early 1970s and will be an instant favorite at the next family reunion! Be sure to keep the dessert chilled until ready to serve and when cutting the chocolate delight, wipe your knife between each cut to keep the layers clean. Let's bring this old favorite back!

———

1. Preheat the oven to 350°F and prepare a 9 x 13-inch pan with baking spray.

2. In a medium mixing bowl, combine the melted butter, pecans, and flour.

3. Press the mixture into the prepared pan and bake for 15 minutes.

4. Remove from the oven and let cool slightly.

5. In the bowl of a stand mixer, fitted with the paddle attachment, combine the cream cheese and confectioner's sugar and mix until creamy. Add in half of the Cool Whip® and mix to combine.

6. Spread the cream cheese mixture on top of the cooled crust.

7. Add the instant pudding and milk to the stand mixer bowl. Switch to the whisk attachment and whisk until well combined and smooth.

8. Dollop and spread the pudding mixture on top of the cream cheese layer.

9. Top with the remaining Cool Whip®. Cover and chill overnight before serving.

CRUST

Baking spray

¾ cup (1½ sticks) unsalted butter, melted

1 cup chopped pecans

1½ cups all-purpose flour

FILLING

8 ounces cream cheese, at room temperature

1 cup confectioners' sugar

1 (16-ounce) carton Cool Whip®, divided

2 (3.9-ounce) packages instant chocolate pudding

3 cups whole milk

PREP TIME: 30-35 minutes | BAKE TIME: 15 minutes
CHILL TIME: at least 12 hours

HERB TOMATO SALAD
{SERVES 8}

When preparing this recipe, you will want to use the chiffonade technique to slice the basil. To do this, stack the basil leaves, roll them, and then thinly slice the rolled leaves. This will create thin ribbons perfect for the tomato salad.

⅓ cup extra-virgin olive oil

¼ cup loosely packed fresh basil, prepared as basil chiffonade

1 teaspoon minced garlic

8 medium heirloom tomatoes (or 4 large tomatoes)

1 Vidalia onion, thinly sliced and separated into rings

Kosher salt, to taste

Freshly ground black pepper, to taste

1. Mix the oil, basil, and garlic in a large mixing bowl to make the dressing.

2. Core and cut the tomatoes into wedges.

3. Toss the tomato wedges in the bowl with the dressing.

4. Add in the sliced onion and stir gently to combine. Sprinkle generously with salt and pepper.

5. Toss gently for a final time and serve at room temperature.

PREP TIME: 15-20 minutes
Pictured on page 73

BAKED CHICKEN NUGGETS
{MAKES 50 NUGGETS}

Chicken nuggets are no longer just for the kids. These baked chicken nuggets have been brought up a notch with the added seasonings and Parmesan cheese. Of course, these can be dipped in ketchup, but a great alternative would be a small dish of warmed marinara sauce.

Cooking spray

2 to 3 pounds boneless, skinless chicken breasts

2 cups fine, dry plain bread crumbs

1 cup grated Parmesan cheese

1 heaping tablespoon dried thyme leaves

1 heaping tablespoon dried basil leaves

1 ½ teaspoons kosher salt

1 cup (2 sticks) unsalted butter, melted

1. Preheat the oven to 400°F and prepare two sheet pans with cooking spray.

2. Cut the chicken into 1 ½-inch cubes and set aside.

3. In a large bowl, combine the bread crumbs, Parmesan, fresh herbs, and seasonings.

4. Dip the chicken cubes first into the melted butter and then into the bread crumb mixture.

5. Place the breaded chicken nuggets on the prepared sheet pans.

6. Bake for 20 minutes and remove the pans from the oven. Using tongs, flip the nuggets.

7. Return the pans to the oven and bake for another 15 to 20 minutes, or until a thermometer inserted in the thickest part of the nuggets reads 165°F.

8. Remove the pans from the oven and serve immediately.

| PREP TIME: 30-35 minutes | BAKE TIME: 35-40 minutes

CORN SALAD
{ S E R V E S 4 }

A refreshing cool salad, perfect for those hot summer days. This is a great recipe to prepare ahead of time and have ready in the refrigerator for whenever your guests arrive.

———

1. In a large bowl, mix the cooked corn, green bell pepper, and celery.

2. In a separate bowl, whisk together the vinegar and oil. Then whisk in the sugar, green onions, parsley, and seasonings. Whisk until the dressing comes together.

3. Pour the dressing over the corn mixture and stir to combine.

4. Cover the corn salad and refrigerate for at least 8 hours before serving.

PREP TIME: 10 minutes | CHILL TIME: 8 hours

16 ounces fresh or frozen corn, cooked and drained

⅔ cup chopped green bell pepper

⅓ cup finely chopped celery

⅓ cup white wine vinegar

⅓ cup vegetable oil

¼ cup granulated sugar

2 green onions, chopped

2 tablespoons chopped fresh flat-leaf parsley

¾ teaspoon Lawry's® Seasoned Salt

¼ teaspoon garlic powder

APPLE SPINACH SALAD
{ S E R V E S 4 T O 6 }

A quick and easy salad to toss together for those busy summer nights. The Cosmic Crisp® apple will add a refreshing and great bite to the salad. This is so different, delicious, and colorful!

———

1. Place the baby spinach in a large bowl. Season the greens lightly with salt and pepper.

2. Mix in the chopped apple, cashews, and dried cranberries.

3. In a cruet or jar, mix the sugar, vegetable oil, and red wine vinegar. Shake until well blended. Add in the celery salt and shake to combine.

4. Pour as much of the dressing as desired over the salad, tossing gently. Leftovers can be stored in an airtight container and refrigerated. Serve salad immediately after dressing.

PREP TIME: 10-15 minutes

12 ounces fresh baby spinach

Kosher salt, to taste

Freshly ground black pepper, to taste

1 Cosmic Crisp® apple, chopped (Granny Smith or Honeycrisp can be substituted, if preferred)

½ cup salted cashews, chopped

¼ cup dried cranberries

¼ cup granulated sugar

¼ cup vegetable oil

2 tablespoons red wine vinegar

¼ teaspoon celery salt

EASY TORTONI COCONUT MACAROON ICE CREAM
{MAKES 1½ QUARTS ICE CREAM}

8 coconut macaroon cookies
(best from a bakery, but crisp
packaged coconut macaroons
can be substituted)

1½ quarts vanilla ice cream,
softened

⅓ cup ground roasted
unsalted almonds

2 tablespoons amaretto
liqueur

1 tablespoon grenadine

Cherries, optional

Whipped cream, optional

Truly one of the easiest desserts to make. When you are looking for the ingredients, check the bulk section in the grocery store to find roasted, unsalted whole almonds. You can use the whole almonds and grind them in a food processor. Allow plenty of time for the ice cream to refreeze before serving (to adults only!).

1. Crush most of the cookies in a food processor. Leave a few of the cookies in bigger pieces.

2. In a large bowl, stir cookies, ice cream, ground almonds, amaretto, and grenadine together. Continue stirring until well combined.

3. Refreeze the ice cream in the freezer for at least 2 hours.

4. When ready to serve, top with a cherry, whipped cream, and a lace cookie (page 224) if desired.

PREP TIME: 5 minutes | CHILL TIME: at least 2 hours

GRAHAM CRACKER COOKIES
{MAKES 50 COOKIES}

Nothing says summer like s'mores, but what to do with the extra boxes of graham crackers at the end of the season? Make these cookies! Quick and easy to make, and you can even let the kids help. Remember this recipe for a great teacher gift!

Cooking spray

1 (14.4-ounce) box
graham crackers

1 cup (2 sticks) unsalted
butter

1 cup firmly packed dark
brown sugar

1 cup chopped pecans

1. Preheat the oven to 400°F and prepare a large, rimmed sheet pan with cooking spray.

2. Cover the bottom of the baking sheet with graham crackers. Set aside.

3. In a heavy-bottomed saucepan set over medium heat, melt the butter and add in the brown sugar. Bring to a boil for 3 minutes, stirring constantly. Remove from heat.

4. Add in the chopped pecans and immediately pour over the graham crackers, spreading quickly but evenly.

5. Place in the oven and bake for 5 minutes. Cool completely and break into pieces.

PREP TIME: 5 minutes | BAKE TIME: 5 minutes

WHOLE WHEAT ROLLS

{MAKES 1 (9 X 13-INCH) PAN}

Always save room for bread at the table! These whole wheat rolls are a great alternative to the classic dinner rolls. This recipe is large enough to serve a crowd, but don't worry if you have leftovers. Store any leftovers at room temperature and use them for a slider bun, or warm them in the oven to accompany dinner the next night.

---

1. Prepare a 14-inch cast iron skillet or rimmed sheet pan with cooking spray.

2. Sift the flour and yeast into the bowl of a stand mixer fitted with the paddle attachment.

3. Heat the milk, water, oil, sugar, and salt in a saucepan over medium heat until very warm, about 115°F. Add the warm liquid all at once to the flour-yeast mixture.

4. Beat at medium speed just until smooth.

5. Add in the whole wheat flour in increments. Add flour until a soft dough forms. Let stand for 12 to 15 minutes.

6. Roll the dough into balls about the size of golf balls and place onto the prepared sheet pan or skillet. The rolls should be touching so they rise up instead of out.

7. Place the pan in a warm place, cover the dough with a tea towel, and let rise for about 1 hour, or until the rolls have doubled in size.

8. Preheat the oven to 350°F about halfway through the rise time.

9. Bake for 20 minutes, or until lightly browned on top. Once the rolls come out of the oven, brush softened butter over the tops. Serve warm.

Cooking spray

2 cups all-purpose flour

2 (¼-ounce) packages dry active yeast

1 cup whole milk

¾ cup water

½ cup vegetable oil

¼ cup granulated sugar

1 tablespoon kosher salt

2½ to 3 cups whole wheat flour, as needed

Salted butter, softened, as needed

PREP TIME: 1 hour 30 minutes | BAKE TIME: 20 minutes

PINEAPPLE CHEESE BALL

{MAKES 1 CHEESE BALL,
24 APPETIZER SERVINGS}

A sweet twist on the cheese ball. Keep in mind the time needed for the cheese ball to chill and factor that into the schedule of preparation for your event. It can always be made a day or two ahead of time to save you time later!

16 ounces cream cheese, softened

1 (8-ounce) can crushed pineapple in juice, drained

¼ cup finely chopped green bell pepper

2 tablespoons finely chopped Vidalia onion

1 teaspoon Lawry's® Seasoned Salt

½ cup pecans, chopped

1 pineapple, for garnish and serving

Crackers, for serving

1. Beat the cream cheese, crushed pineapple, green pepper, onion, and Lawry's® in the bowl of a stand mixer fitted with the paddle attachment.

2. Remove from the bowl and form the cream cheese mixture into a ball.

3. Roll the cream cheese ball in the chopped pecans so the entire outside is covered.

4. Tightly wrap the cheese ball in plastic wrap and chill for at least 2 hours.

5. When ready to serve, trim the sides of the pineapple. Cut the peeled pineapple into chunks but save the green top. Unwrap the cheese ball and place the green top on the cheese ball to give it the appearance of a pineapple.

6. Grill the pineapple chunks to serve on the side of the cheese ball along with the crackers.

PREP TIME: 10-12 minutes | CHILL TIME: 2 hours

LEMON CHEESECAKE SQUARES

{ MAKES 1 (9 X 13-INCH) PAN }

Possibly one of the most perfect summer desserts, both sweet and tart. These cheesecake squares are so refreshing but also so easy to make. Do not be scared off by cheesecake in the name. Just a warning now, one batch might not be enough!

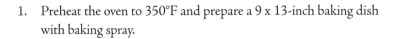

1. Preheat the oven to 350°F and prepare a 9 x 13-inch baking dish with baking spray.

2. Mix the condensed milk, grated lemon peel, and lemon juice in a mixing bowl. Set aside.

3. In the bowl of a stand mixer, cream the butter and sugar until fluffy, about 3 to 5 minutes.

4. Add in the flour, baking powder, salt, and rolled oats to creamed butter mixture. Mix until crumbly.

5. Firmly press half of the crumb mixture into the bottom of the prepared baking dish.

6. Pour the sweetened condensed milk mixture on top of the crust. Cover with the remaining crumb mixture and press down gently.

7. Bake for 25 to 30 minutes, or until brown around the edges. Allow to cool.

8. Chill in the refrigerator completely before cutting. This recipe is best if you are able to allow the cheesecake squares to chill overnight before cutting and serving.

Baking spray

3 (14-ounce) cans sweetened condensed milk

1 tablespoon freshly grated lemon peel

1½ cups freshly squeezed lemon juice

1 cup (2 sticks) unsalted butter, at room temperature

1½ cups firmly packed light brown sugar

2¼ cups all-purpose flour

1½ teaspoons baking powder

⅓ teaspoon kosher salt

1½ cups old fashioned rolled oats

PREP TIME: 35 minutes | BAKE TIME: 25-30 minutes
CHILL TIME: At least 12 hours

GOUDA CRESCENTS
{MAKES 24 CRESCENTS}

A delicious Gouda filling wrapped in warm puff pastry makes an extremely appetizing small bite for your friends and family. The optional sauces can add either a little sweetness or a little heat. Feel free to increase the cayenne pepper in the filling as well, if the father you are cooking for likes food on the spicier side!

***

1. Preheat the oven to 325°F and line a sheet pan with parchment paper.

2. In a heavy-bottomed pan, melt the butter over medium heat. Sauté the green onions until soft. Remove from heat and stir in the cayenne.

3. Add in the cheese and mix well.

4. Using a 2¼-inch biscuit cutter, cut the pastry sheet into medium-sized rounds. Brush each round with egg.

5. Add a teaspoon of the cheese mixture to each pastry round.

6. Fold pastry rounds over in half, creating a half-moon shape, and seal the edges with a fork. Place on the prepared sheet pan.

7. Bake for 20 to 25 minutes, or until golden brown.

8. Before enjoying, you can choose to add a drizzle of warmed apple jelly or a drizzle of hot honey. Spoon the apple jelly into a small saucepan set over medium-low heat and warm just enough that it is able to be drizzled. If serving with the hot honey, see recipe below.

HOT HONEY

1. In a small saucepan set over medium-low heat, stir together the honey and red pepper flakes.

2. Heat the honey until you see bubbles around the edges of the pan; do not let it come to a simmer.

3. Remove the pan from heat and stir the hot pepper vinegar into the honey. Let the honey sit for 5 minutes so the red pepper flakes have time to infuse.

4. Strain the honey through a fine mesh sieve into a clean glass jar. Let cool completely before sealing the jar.

5. Store at room temperature until needed.

CRESCENTS

2 tablespoons unsalted butter

1 cup chopped green onions

⅛ teaspoon cayenne pepper

1 cup (4 ounces) shredded Gouda cheese

1 (17.3-ounce) box puff pastry, defrosted

1 large egg, beaten

Apple jelly, optional

Hot honey, optional (see below)

HOT HONEY

1 cup honey

2 tablespoons red pepper flakes

1 teaspoon hot pepper vinegar

PREP TIME: 35-40 minutes | BAKE TIME: 20-25 minutes

PORK

1 tablespoon extra-virgin olive oil

1 to 1½ pounds pork loin, cut into 1-inch cubes

1 orange bell pepper, sliced

1 Vidalia onion, thinly sliced

1 (14-ounce) can bean sprouts

1 (20-ounce) can pineapple chunks, in juice, drained (reserve ¼ cup juice for the sauce)

SAUCE

½ cup ketchup

¼ cup granulated sugar

¼ cup pineapple juice (from canned pineapple)

¼ cup white wine vinegar

¼ cup reduced sodium soy sauce

1 tablespoon Worcestershire sauce

1 teaspoon kosher salt

1 tablespoon cornstarch mixed with ½ cup of water

Rice, for serving

BITSY'S SWEET AND SOUR PORK
{SERVES 4 TO 6}

A classic Chinese takeout dish that you can now make at home! This is a great Father's Day dinner that everyone in the family can enjoy. Some of the best parts of this dish are the warm pineapple chunks covered in a sweet and tangy sauce. This was one of the first recipes that was given to me by my sister, Bitsy.

———

1. Heat the olive oil in a large skillet set over medium heat. Add in the cubed pork and cook until the pork is browned on all sides, about 5 minutes. Remove the pork from the pan and set aside.

2. Add the bell pepper, onion, and bean sprouts to skillet. Continue to cook until the bell pepper and onion begin to soften, about 5 to 6 minutes. Drain any excess oil or grease.

3. Pour in the pineapple chunks and return the pork to the pan. Turn the heat to medium-low and allow the mixture to cook for another 5 minutes.

4. In a small mixing bowl, combine all sauce ingredients except for the cornstarch. Mix well with a whisk.

5. While stirring, add in the cornstarch slurry to the mixing bowl with the sauce.

6. Pour the sauce into the skillet with the pork and vegetables. Stir to combine and raise the heat to medium.

7. Cook until the sauce thickens, and the pork is fully cooked through, about 3 to 5 minutes, or until the pork reaches an internal temperature of 145º F.

8. Serve hot over rice.

PREP TIME: 15-20 minutes | COOK TIME: 20-25 minutes

"THAT" RICE

{ SERVES 8 }

People will be asking for "that" rice recipe—and you'll know exactly which one they are talking about. Baking the rice in the oven is so easy and eliminates the tedious task of constantly watching the rice on the stove. Who knew adding such simple ingredients found in your pantry could add so much flavor!

1. Preheat the oven to 350°F and prepare a 2 ½-quart casserole dish with cooking spray.

2. In a large skillet with tall sides, melt the butter over medium heat. Brown the rice in the butter, about 3 to 5 minutes.

3. Add in the onion soup mix, water, seasonings, and garlic. Mix well.

4. Add in just enough Kitchen Bouquet® to color it nicely, about two dashes. Stir to incorporate.

5. Pour the rice mixture into the prepared casserole dish and bake, covered, for 40 minutes.

6. Remove the dish from the oven, stir, cover, and bake for another 20 minutes.

7. Serve warm.

Cooking spray

3 tablespoons unsalted butter

1½ cups white long grain rice

1 (1-ounce) envelope dry onion soup mix

3¾ cups water

Kosher salt, to taste

Freshly ground black pepper, to taste

2 cloves garlic, minced

Kitchen Bouquet®, as desired (optional)

PREP TIME: 10 minutes | COOK TIME: 1 hour 5 minutes

CHOCOLATE DREAM PIE

{MAKES 1 (9-INCH) PIE}

This pie can be made to your personal preference by choosing how much chocolate you incorporate in the filling and whether you add almonds or coconut to the crust. A perfect dessert to help everyone cool off after a day by the pool.

Cooking spray

CRUST

2 cups old fashioned Quaker Oats®

1 cup toasted coconut or sliced almonds, depending on personal preference

½ cup (1 stick) margarine, melted

¼ cup firmly packed light brown sugar

FILLING

1 (16-ounce) container Cool Whip®, thawed

4 to 6 (1.45-ounce) Hershey's® bars (with almonds), melted and cooled slightly

1. Preheat the oven to 350°F and prepate a rimmed sheet pan with cooking spray. Spread the oatmeal out in a single layer on the prepared pan. Bake for 5 to 7 minutes, stirring occasionally.

2. Raise the oven temperature to 375°F.

3. In a large mixing bowl, combine the oatmeal, toasted almonds or coconut, margarine, and brown sugar. Press the mixture into the bottom of the pie dish and bake for 10 minutes. Push the sides of the crust up as soon as it comes out of the oven. Set the crust aside to cool.

4. In a large bowl, fold the Cool Whip® and the melted chocolate bars together. Use as much of the melted chocolate as you desire; I prefer a more marbled look.

5. Dollop the chocolate mixture and spread evenly into the cooled pie crust.

6. Wrap the pie lightly with plastic wrap and place in the freezer until ready to serve. You may have to let the pie sit out for a few minutes before slicing it.

PREP TIME: 25 minutes | CHILL TIME: At least 1 hour

CHICKEN CACCIATORE

{SERVES 6}

This is my husband Andy's recipe. I remember the first time he made it I thought, "You should be cooking every night!" He does a lot of the cooking now. The ingredient list might look long but it will all be worth it when you take a bite of this rustic, heartwarming dish. I like to serve the chicken over a bed of rice, but you can use pasta, mashed potatoes, or a bed of steamed vegetables.

———

1. Generously season the chicken thighs with salt and pepper. Dredge each chicken thigh in flour.

2. Heat the oil and butter in a large skillet set over medium-high heat. Add in the chicken thighs and cook for 3 to 5 minutes per side. Remove the chicken from the skillet and set aside.

3. Add the chopped bacon to the skillet and cook until crisp. Remove the bacon from the pan and set aside.

4. Add the onion and mushrooms to the pan with the bacon drippings and sauté over medium heat for about 5 minutes. Add in the garlic and cook for another 30 seconds.

5. Stir in the canned tomatoes with the juice, pimentos and pimento juice, vermouth, chicken broth, bay leaves, and remaining seasonings. Bring to a boil.

6. Add the chicken thighs and cooked bacon back into the pan. Reduce the heat to low and simmer, covered, for about 45 to 55 minutes, stirring occasionally, until a thermometer inserted in the middle of the chicken reads 165°F.

7. Remove the bay leaves and serve immediately over the cooked basmati rice.

8. Garnish with shaved Parmesan cheese.

PREP TIME: 15-20 minutes | COOK TIME: 1 hour 15 minutes

6 bone-in chicken thighs

Kosher salt

Freshly ground black pepper

1½ cups all-purpose flour

2 tablespoons extra-virgin olive oil

2 tablespoons unsalted butter

3 slices uncooked bacon, chopped

½ Vidalia onion, chopped

8 ounces fresh baby Bella mushrooms, sliced

3 garlic cloves, minced

1 (14.5-ounce) can diced tomatoes, undrained

1 (4-ounce) jar pimentos, diced with juice reserved

⅓ cup dry vermouth

½ cup chicken broth

3 bay leaves

1 teaspoon dried thyme

1 teaspoon dried oregano

½ teaspoon crushed red pepper flakes

Basmati rice, cooked, for serving

Shaved Parmesan cheese, as garnish

BROILED CHICKEN WITH GRAVY

{ SERVES 4 }

This is another recipe that I'm going to walk you through like I'm standing with you. The technique is almost as important as the ingredients. My son Daniel always requested this for his birthday.

Cooking spray

4 chicken breasts, bone-in and skin-on (you can use bone-in chicken legs and thighs if you prefer)

Morton® Nature's Seasons® Salt, to taste

4 tablespoons unsalted butter, divided

1 to 2 tablespoons cornstarch

2 to 4 tablespoons cold water

Dash of Kitchen Bouquet®

White rice, for serving

1. Preheat the oven to 325°F and prepare a 9 x 13-inch baking pan with cooking spray.

2. Pat the chicken dry with paper towels and season both sides with the Nature's Seasons® Salt. Place the chicken in the prepared pan, skin-side up.

3. Spray the chicken lightly with cooking spray and dot with half of the butter.

4. Place the pan in the oven and bake for 30 minutes.

5. After 30 minutes, remove the pan from the oven and dot the chicken with remaining butter. Place the pan back in the oven and bake for an additional 10 to 15 minutes, or until a thermometer inserted in the thickest part of the chicken reads 165°F.

6. Once done, remove the pan from the oven and place the chicken pieces on a platter. Loosely cover with foil to keep warm. Transfer the drippings to a small saucepan.

7. Mix the cornstarch and cold water in a 1:2 ratio of cornstarch to water.

8. Heat the drippings over medium-high heat and bring to a light boil. Pour half of the cornstarch slurry into the drippings, whisking until it begins to thicken, about 3 minutes. Add more of the cornstarch slurry if needed.

9. Add a dash of the Kitchen Bouquet® for browning and flavor (it may only take a drop). Stir to combine and turn the heat to low.

10. Turn the oven to broil.

11. Once the gravy is complete and you are almost ready to serve, move the top rack in the oven about 4 inches from the broiler. Place the chicken pieces back in the baking pan and broil for about 3 to 4 minutes, or until desired crispness and browning is achieved.

12. Serve on a bed of white rice and pour gravy over each.

PREP TIME: 10-15 minutes | COOK TIME: 45-50 minutes

COUNTRY-FRIED STEAK WITH MILK GRAVY

{ SERVES 6 }

A Southern classic and my son John's favorite. The secret to the perfect breading on the steak is the mixture of self-rising flour and rice flour. I love the touch of heat that the hot sauce adds!

---

6 pieces cubed steak

Morton® Nature's Seasons® Salt

Canola oil, for frying

1 cup half-and-half, divided (use more as needed for the gravy)

½ teaspoon Tabasco® hot sauce

1 cup self-rising flour

1 cup rice flour

Chicken stock, if needed

1 teaspoon Kitchen Bouquet®

Mashed potatoes, for serving

1. Season both sides of the cubed steak with Nature's Seasons Salt®.

2. Prepare a large cast iron skillet with about ½ inch of canola oil and heat to 350°F over medium-high heat.

3. In a small bowl, mix ½ cup half-and-half and the Tabasco®. In a separate mixing bowl, combine the self-rising flour and rice flour.

4. Dip the steak pieces in the half-and-half mixture, then in the flour mixture, shaking off any excess.

5. Place in the skillet and let brown well before flipping, about 3 minutes per side.

6. Once all 6 pieces have been fried, remove most of the oil from the pan, leaving just the drippings that have browned.

7. Return the skillet to the stove over medium heat and heat the drippings slowly while adding in the remaining half-and-half until you achieve your desired thickness for the gravy.

8. To thin, add chicken stock, if desired. Add Kitchen Bouquet® to the finished gravy and stir well.

9. Serve the steak on a bed of mashed potatoes with the gravy poured over each.

PREP TIME: 10 minutes | COOK TIME: 25-30 minutes

Pictured on page 95

BRAISED LAMB SHANKS

{ SERVES 6 }

An elegant main entree served on a bed of mashed potatoes or polenta. This dish is my son Cord's favorite and one I have made on *The Very Vera Show* when I featured my three sons' favorite dishes.

———

1. Heat 2 tablespoons olive oil in a heavy skillet with tall sides over medium heat, and sauté the celery, onion, carrots, and garlic until vegetables begin to brown, about 20 minutes.

2. Add in the tomato paste and cook for 2 minutes longer. Add beef broth to deglaze the pan and bring to a boil.

3. Remove from the heat and add the rosemary, thyme, and lemon peel.

4. Pour mixture into a large roasting pan. Set aside.

5. Preheat the oven to 325°F.

6. Sprinkle the lamb shanks with salt and pepper. Dredge lightly with flour.

7. Sauté lamb shanks in 2 to 4 tablespoons of olive oil in a large skillet set over medium heat until browned on both sides. Remove from heat.

8. Place the browned shanks on top of the vegetable mixture in the roasting pan.

9. Deglaze the skillet with the red wine, scraping up all of the brown bits. Pour wine mixture over lamb.

10. Cover and bake in the oven for 2 hours. Remove the lid and bake for 30 minutes longer, or until shanks are browned and tender.

11. Serve immediately with mashed potatoes or polenta.

PREP TIME: 25 minutes | COOK TIME: 3 hours

4 to 6 tablespoons extra-virgin olive oil, divided

1 cup sliced celery, cut in ½-inch slices

2 medium Vidalia onions, chopped

3 to 4 large carrots, peeled and diced

6 to 8 large garlic cloves, minced

2 tablespoons tomato paste

2 (14.5-ounce) cans beef broth

2 tablespoons finely chopped fresh rosemary

3 to 4 large sprigs fresh thyme, tied together

2 teaspoons freshly grated lemon peel

6 large lamb shanks, excess fat and silver skin removed

Pinch kosher salt

Pinch freshly ground black pepper

All-purpose flour, for dusting

2 ½ cups dry red wine

Mashed potatoes or polenta, for serving

Pictured on page 95

SOUTHERN CHOPPED SALAD

{SERVES 4}

A classic salad with almost all Southern ingredients! This is a delicious side salad, but it can also make a great main dish if you are looking for something on the lighter side. Every bite of this salad will have a different ingredient that will keep you going back for more!

SALAD

8 ounces thick center-cut bacon, uncooked

8 ounces baby arugula (can use spring mix if preferred)

1 Cosmic Crisp® apple, diced

½ cup toasted pecan halves, coarsely chopped

½ cup dried cranberries

½ cup white shoepeg corn

½ cup fresh green beans, blanched and chopped

½ cup shredded Swiss and Gruyère cheese blend

DRESSING

2 tablespoons apple cider vinegar

1 small shallot, roughly chopped

½ teaspoon freshly grated orange peel

1 tablespoon freshly squeezed orange juice

1 teaspoon prepared yellow mustard

1 tablespoon pure maple syrup

Kosher salt, to taste

¼ teaspoon freshly ground black pepper

1 tablespoon reserved bacon grease

⅓ cup pecan oil

1. Preheat the oven to 400°F and line a sheet pan with foil. Place a baking rack on the foiled sheet pan.

2. Lay the bacon slices on the rack. Cook in the oven for 20 to 25 minutes, or until the bacon is cooked and crispy. Allow the bacon to cool and reserve 1 tablespoon bacon grease for the salad dressing.

3. While the bacon is cooling, make the apple cider dressing.

4. In a blender, combine all dressing ingredients except for the pecan oil. Blend until combined. With the blender on low, slowly pour in the pecan oil. Continue to blend until fully combined.

5. To assemble the salad, toss the arugula, apple, pecans, cranberries, corn, green beans, and shredded cheese together in a large salad bowl.

6. Chop the cooled bacon into large pieces. Add the bacon pieces to the salad bowl.

7. Dress the salad with as much of the vinaigrette as desired and toss just before serving. Leftover vinaigrette can be stored in an airtight container in the refrigerator.

COOK TIME: 20-25 minutes | PREP TIME: 30 minutes

MACARONI SALAD

{MAKES 8 (1-CUP) SERVINGS}

I was given this recipe as a newlywed with a note to bring it for summer BBQs or any gathering. You're going to love it, too!

1. Cook the elbow macaroni according to package directions, then drain, and let cool.

2. In a separate small bowl, mix the mayonnaise, lemon juice, apple cider vinegar, and seasonings.

3. Once macaroni has cooled, place in a large bowl and add in the cabbage, carrot, green bell pepper, and green onion. Mix well.

4. Pour in the mayonnaise dressing and gently toss until combined. Cover and chill for at least 2 to 3 hours before serving.

5. Salt and pepper to taste and enjoy! Any leftovers can be stored in the refrigerator and will last for several days.

*Angel Hair Coleslaw from the grocery store can be used but I prefer to thinly slice my own cabbage with a very sharp knife.

PREP TIME: 25 minutes | CHILL TIME: 2-3 hours

8 ounces dry elbow macaroni

1 cup Hellmann's® mayonnaise

3 tablespoons freshly squeezed lemon juice

1 teaspoon apple cider vinegar

1½ teaspoons dry mustard

1½ teaspoons granulated sugar

1 teaspoon kosher salt

1 teaspoon celery seed

Pinch garlic powder

3 cups finely shredded green cabbage* (not grated)

1 cup coarsely shredded carrot

½ cup finely chopped green bell pepper

2 tablespoons sliced green onions

Kosher salt, to taste

Freshly ground black pepper, to taste

JONES' SALAD DRESSING
{MAKES ½ CUP}

My husband, Andy, has always been "Jones" to me. He is affectionately known as Papa Jones and all of our children know how to make this dressing. It's a delicious salad dressing that uses a lot of ingredients that are most likely already in your pantry!

1½ teaspoons granulated sugar

¼ teaspoon kosher salt

⅛ teaspoon freshly ground black pepper

3 tablespoons plus 1½ teaspoons canola oil

2 tablespoons apple cider vinegar

1 tablespoon plus 1½ teaspoons balsamic vinegar

1 tablespoon plus

2 tablespoons blue cheese

2 green onions, chopped

1. In a wooden salad bowl, add the sugar, salt, and pepper. Stir with the back of a large plastic serving spoon to slightly crush the seasoning.

2. Add in the canola oil, apple cider vinegar, and balsamic vinegar and continue to combine using the back of the spoon.

3. Add the blue cheese to the bowl and mash the crumbles into small pieces with the spoon.

4. Add in the green onions and stir well to combine.

5. Store in a cruet or an airtight jar in the refrigerator.

PREP TIME: 5-10 minutes

VERA'S TOMATO VINAIGRETTE
{MAKES 4 CUPS}

This recipe makes a large batch of dressing, but it can easily be cut in half if needed. A fantastic salad dressing to make and keep on hand in the refrigerator.

1 cup Heinz® Chili Sauce

1 cup vegetable oil

1 cup apple cider vinegar

1 cup granulated sugar

1 small Vidalia onion, grated

1 teaspoon kosher salt

1 teaspoon freshly ground black pepper

1 teaspoon paprika

1. In a quart jar, combine all ingredients and shake well.

2. Store the jar in the refrigerator for weeks.

NOTE: This dressing is great for a basic tossed salad with sectioned grapefruit, sliced red onion, sliced avocado, and crumbled feta cheese.

PREP TIME: 10-15 minutes

RICE CASSEROLE
{MAKES 4 (1-CUP) SERVINGS}

My high school boyfriend's mother gave me this recipe and I still like to prepare it to this day. She was a great cook! This dish is best when served warm, so if you plan to take it to an outdoor BBQ, wrap the dish in aluminum foil when it comes out of the oven. The wrapped dish can be stored in a cooler (without ice) to help keep the dish hot before serving.

Cooking spray

1 extra-large chicken bouillon cube or 2 teaspoons Better Than Bouillon® Roasted Chicken Base

2 cups hot water

Kosher salt, to taste

4 tablespoons unsalted butter

1 cup Ben's Original® rice, uncooked

½ cup chopped celery

½ cup chopped green onions

½ cup slivered almonds

1. Preheat the oven to 350°F and prepare an 8 x 8-inch casserole dish with cooking spray.

2. In a small bowl, dissolve the bouillon cubes (or Better Than Bouillon) in the hot water. Taste the chicken broth and salt to taste.

3. In a large skillet set over medium heat, melt the butter. Add in the rice and toast the rice until light golden brown in color, about 3 to 5 minutes. Pour in the chicken broth from the previous step and stir well to combine.

4. Transfer the rice and liquid to a casserole dish and cover. Bake for 30 minutes.

5. Remove from the oven and stir in the celery, green onions, and almonds. Return to the oven and bake, covered, for another 30 minutes.

6. Serve warm and enjoy!

PREP TIME: 15-20 minutes | COOK TIME: 1 hour

CORN CASSEROLE

{MAKES A 2½-QUART CASSEROLE DISH}

Summer is the perfect time to use fresh corn whenever possible. If you are looking for something other than corn on the cob, then this corn casserole is the dish for you.

---

1. Preheat the oven to 350°F and prepare a 2½-quart casserole dish with cooking spray.

2. In a large saucepan set over medium heat, melt 2 tablespoons unsalted butter. Add in the chopped fresh corn and lightly sauté.

3. Add in the canned corn and milk; stir to combine. Cook the milk and corn until warm. Add in the flour and whisk until thickened.

4. Add in the pimento and season with salt and pepper. Turn the heat to low and slowly whisk in the eggs to combine.

5. Add in 1 cup of the crushed saltine crackers and mix thoroughly.

6. Pour the corn mixture into the prepared casserole dish. Top with the remaining crushed saltine crackers. Melt the remaining tablespoon of butter in the microwave and drizzle the corn and crackers with the melted butter.

7. Bake for 15 to 20 minutes, or until casserole is heated through and the crackers on top are golden brown.

Cooking spray

3 tablespoons unsalted butter, divided

1 cup finely chopped fresh corn

2 (14.75-ounce) cans cream style sweet corn

1 cup whole milk

2 tablespoons all-purpose flour

3 tablespoons chopped pimento

¾ teaspoon kosher salt

Freshly ground black pepper, to taste

2 large eggs, beaten

2 cups coarsely crushed saltine crackers, divided

PREP TIME: 30 minutes | BAKE TIME: 15-20 minutes

PICKLE-BRINED FRIED CHICKEN

{SERVES 3 TO 4}

For this recipe, you can choose to use the boneless chicken breasts, or you can brine and fry bone-in chicken pieces. If you're looking for other ideas on how to use the nuggets, try making mini buttermilk biscuits (you can find a buttermilk biscuit recipe in *The VeryVera Cookbook: Recipes from My Table*, page 36) and make mini chicken biscuit sandwiches for brunch!

---

1 pound boneless, skinless chicken breasts

1 cup dill pickle juice

1½ cups whole milk, divided

Peanut oil, for frying

1 large egg

1¼ cups all-purpose flour

1 teaspoon confectioners' sugar

½ teaspoon garlic powder

Kosher salt, to taste

Freshly ground black pepper, to taste

1. Cut the chicken into bite-sized pieces, about 1 inch long. Place the chicken in a large resealable plastic bag and add in the dill pickle juice and ½ cup milk. Let the chicken brine in the milk mixture in the refrigerator overnight.

2. The next day, drain the chicken pieces.

3. Heat a large pot with about 2 inches of peanut oil (or use a fryer).

4. In a large mixing bowl, combine the remaining 1 cup milk and the egg. Add the marinated chicken and toss gently to coat, draining off the excess egg mixture if needed.

5. In a separate mixing bowl, whisk together the flour, confectioners' sugar, garlic powder, salt, and pepper.

6. Remove the chicken from the milk mixture and add the chicken pieces into the flour mixture to coat evenly.

7. When the oil has reached 350°F, add a few nuggets at a time to the hot oil. Cook until the chicken is browned and crispy, about 3 to 4 minutes per nugget. Remove the cooked chicken nuggets from the hot oil using a slotted spoon and drain on a paper towel-lined plate. Check the chicken nuggets with a thermometer to make sure the thickest part of each nugget reads at least 165°F. Return any nuggets to the oil if they need to cook longer. Repeat with the remaining chicken nuggets.

8. If needed, place the chicken nuggets on a sheet pan to brown or keep warm in the oven.

9. Serve hot with condiments of your choice.

PREP TIME: 15 minutes (plus time for the chicken to brine overnight)
COOK TIME: 15 minutes

PEACH ICE CREAM

{MAKES 2½ TO 3 QUARTS}

Summer in the South means fresh peaches, and nothing tastes better on a hot, humid day than fresh peach ice cream. This recipe makes plenty of ice cream to keep in the freezer for whenever the craving hits. Top with whipped cream or more peach slices and enjoy!

---

1. In a large blender or food processor, combine the eggs and sugar. Blend until thoroughly mixed.

2. Add in the evaporated milk, whipping cream, almond extract, vanilla extract, and peaches. Blend until the peaches are broken up and the mixture is mostly smooth (a few larger chunks of peaches is fine).

3. Transfer half of the ice cream mixture to an electric 2-quart ice cream machine. Place the remaining half in the refrigerator until ready to churn. Note: you may need to freeze the bowl of the machine before churning the remaining half.

4. Churn the ice cream for about 20 minutes, or until done. Repeat with the remaining ice cream mixture.

5. Place the ice cream in the freezer for at least 3 hours before serving to allow the ice cream to set.

NOTE: Have fun with the kids and make peach ice cream sandwiches. As your sandwich component, you can use slices of pound cake or even sugar cookies!

PREP TIME: 15 minutes | CHILL TIME: 3 hours

5 large eggs

2 cups granulated sugar

1 (12-ounce) can evaporated milk

1 pint heavy whipping cream

¼ teaspoon almond extract

1 teaspoon pure vanilla extract

4 cups sliced peaches, fresh or frozen

PEANUT BUTTER TOFFEE COOKIES

{MAKES 60 COOKIES}

Delicious cookies with a surprise in every bite! My home state of Georgia is known for peanuts; I was even able to visit and learn from some Georgia peanut farmers on an episode of my cooking show, which was such a fun experience! Hope you enjoy these cookies as much as I do!

———

3½ cups all-purpose flour

2 cups old fashioned rolled oats

1 teaspoon baking soda

1 teaspoon kosher salt

2 cups (4 sticks) unsalted butter, at room temperature

1½ cups firmly packed light brown sugar

1 cup creamy peanut butter

4 teaspoons pure vanilla extract

2 large eggs, at room temperature

2 cups honey roasted peanuts

10 ounces peanut butter chips

8 ounces toffee bits

1. In a medium mixing bowl, combine the flour, rolled oats, baking soda, and kosher salt.

2. In the bowl of a stand mixer fitted with the paddle attachment, beat the butter and brown sugar on medium speed for about 3 minutes, or until light and fluffy.

3. Beat in the peanut butter and vanilla extract.

4. Add in the eggs, one at a time, beating until just incorporated.

5. Reduce speed to low, then beat in the flour mixture until just combined. Remove bowl from mixer.

6. Stir in the peanuts, peanut butter chips, and toffee bits by hand. Cover the bowl and refrigerate for at least 2 to 3 hours, or overnight.

7. When ready to bake, preheat the oven to 375°F and line cookie sheets with parchment paper.

8. Pinch the dough to golf ball size and flatten to about ½- to ¾-inch thickness.

9. Freeze the dough on the baking sheets for 10 minutes or until firm.

10. Remove the pans from the freezer and place in the oven. Bake for 12 minutes, or until cookies are lightly browned on the edges.

11. Place the baking sheet on a wire rack and cool for 3 minutes. Remove the cookies from the pan and cool completely on the wire rack before storing.

NOTE: These baked cookies freeze well.

PREP TIME: 30 minutes | CHILL TIME: at least 2-3 hours
COOK TIME: 12 minutes

FOURTH OF JULY POUND CAKE TRIFLE

{MAKES 1 LARGE TRIFLE DISH, 10 SERVINGS}

A picture-worthy dessert that will wow all the guests at the BBQ! The fresh berries are the perfect accompaniment to the pound cake. For this recipe, I used Trip's Lemon Crisp Cake from my first cookbook, but you can also choose to use Lou's Cream Cheese Cake (page 166) or even Betty's Citrus Blueberry Cake (page 155).

---

1. Cube the pound cake into about 1-inch pieces. You will need enough cake cubes to make 3 layers in the trifle dish. Mix together the berries and sugar in a medium mixing bowl. Set aside until ready to assemble.

2. In a large bowl, beat together the pudding mix and whole milk. In the bowl of a stand mixer fitted with the paddle attachment, whip the cream cheese and sweetened condensed milk until smooth and creamy. Add in the heavy cream and vanilla extract. Beat until soft peaks form, about 5 minutes. Fold in the pudding mixture.

3. To assemble the trifle, start with ⅓ of the cake cubes in the bottom of the container. Dollop ⅓ of the custard mixture, then ⅓ of the berry mixture on top. Continue layering cake, custard, and berries until all ingredients are used. (You may have leftover pound cake.)

4. Cover and refrigerate the trifle until ready to serve. This dessert can be made ahead and stored in the refrigerator for up to 24 hours.

PREP TIME: 30 minutes

1 pound cake of choice, we suggest using Trip's Lemon Crisp Cake from *The Very-Vera Cookbook: Recipes from My Table* (page 151)

2 pounds fresh strawberries, sliced with stems removed

12 ounces fresh blueberries

6 ounces fresh raspberries, optional

⅓ cup granulated sugar

1 (5-ounce) package instant French vanilla pudding mix

1½ cups whole milk

8 ounces cream cheese, at room temperature

1 (14-ounce) can sweetened condensed milk

1½ cups heavy whipping cream

1 teaspoon pure vanilla extract

SUN-DRIED TOMATO DIP
{MAKES 2 CUPS}

8 ounces cream cheese, at room temperature

½ cup sour cream

½ cup mayonnaise

¾ teaspoon Tabasco® hot sauce

1 teaspoon kosher salt

¾ teaspoon freshly ground black pepper

¼ cup sun-dried tomatoes in oil, drained and chopped, divided

2 green onions, thinly sliced

Crackers or vegetables, for serving

A dip with a touch of heat, balanced by the sweetness of the sun-dried tomatoes. The chopped sun-dried tomatoes and sliced green onions add texture as well. This dip will last for up to a week when stored in an airtight container in the refrigerator. This is a great addition to a charcuterie board to add more color.

1. In the bowl of a food processor, pulse the cream cheese, sour cream, mayonnaise, Tabasco®, salt, pepper, and most of the sundried tomatoes, until combined. Reserve a few of the chopped tomatoes to mix in later.

2. Add in the green onions and pulse briefly until just combined.

3. Transfer to a mixing bowl and fold in the remaining sun-dried tomatoes with a rubber spatula.

4. Serve with your favorite crackers or vegetables.

PREP TIME: 10-15 minutes

PARMESAN PARTY LOG
{MAKES 11 OUNCES}

8 ounces cream cheese, softened

½ cup freshly shredded Parmesan cheese

½ teaspoon garlic salt

1 tablespoon chopped green bell pepper

1 tablespoon chopped jalapeño, deseeded

2 tablespoons diced pimento

1 tablespoon sliced green onions, as garnish

1 tablespoon chopped parsley, as garnish

Chips, crackers, or vegetables (for serving)

Summer BBQs call for quick and easy appetizers and this cheese log is just that! This appetizer is best kept chilled so if possible either keep this dish inside or keep the serving dish set on top of an ice pack. Enjoy!

1. In a medium mixing bowl, mix the cream cheese, Parmesan, garlic salt, green bell pepper, jalapeño, and pimento.

2. Once the mixture is incorporated, place in the refrigerator and chill for at least 2 hours.

3. After chilling, remove the mixture from the bowl and shape into a log.

4. On a plate, mix together the sliced green onions and chopped parsley. Roll the log in the garnish mixture.

5. Serve with your favorite chips, crackers, or vegetables.

PREP TIME: 5-10 minutes | CHILL TIME: 2 hours

BEAU MONDE VEGETABLE DIP

{MAKES 2 CUPS}

The original name of this recipe is Cauliflower Dip; the original recipe card was actually printed in my first cookbook, *The VeryVera Cookbook: Recipes from My Table* (page 179). Beau Monde seasoning may be difficult to find in your local grocery store. If so, it is available to order online. This dip is great for vegetables or crackers of your choosing.

1. In a large mixing bowl, mix the sour cream and mayonnaise.

2. Add in the seasonings and mix well.

3. Chill for at least 2 hours, or until ready to serve. Serve with cauliflower, squash, celery, carrots, and/or cucumbers.

1 cup sour cream

1 cup Hellmann's® mayonnaise

1 tablespoon dry onion soup mix

1 tablespoon dill weed

1 tablespoon Spice Islands® Beau Monde seasoning

PREP TIME: 5 minutes | CHILL TIME: 2 hours

ROASTED WHITE CORN SALSA

{MAKES 3 CUPS}

You can choose to serve this as a topping or a side dish, either warm or chilled. If you do not have fresh corn to use, frozen corn can be substituted. Roast the frozen corn directly from the freezer.

1. Preheat the oven to 425°F and prepare a baking sheet with cooking spray.

2. Toss the corn with the olive oil and lightly season with salt and pepper, to taste.

3. Spread out in a single layer on a baking sheet and roast for about 10 to 15 minutes, or until lightly browned.

4. Cool the corn and add to a large mixing bowl.

5. Add the remaining ingredients to the mixing bowl with the corn. Stir well to combine.

6. Serve at room temperature or chilled.

7. Store any leftovers in an airtight container in the refrigerator for up to 5 days.

Cooking spray

2 cups sweet white corn, cut from the cob

¼ cup extra-virgin olive oil

Kosher salt, to taste

Freshly ground black pepper, to taste

⅓ cup finely diced red bell pepper

⅓ cup finely diced red onion

1 teaspoon minced serrano pepper, seeded

1 tablespoon sherry vinegar

1 teaspoon freshly squeezed lemon juice

1 teaspoon honey

PREP TIME: 15 minutes | COOK TIME: 10-15 minutes

ROASTED GREEN BEANS

{SERVES 4 TO 6}

When you are making the green beans, it may seem like a lot of brown sugar. But the soy sauce will help cut through the sweetness. The final roast in the oven will help tighten the sauce so it sticks to the green beans. This is a great side dish to serve with the Sweet and Sour Pork (page 88). The beans in this dish are crisp, so for all you Southerners that like your vegetables softer, change the cooking time to 20 to 25 minutes.

---

2 pounds fresh green beans

½ cup (1 stick) salted butter

1 cup firmly packed light brown sugar

¾ teaspoon garlic powder

2 tablespoons reduced sodium soy sauce

1 teaspoon toasted sesame seeds

1. Wash the green beans and prepare by cutting off the tips.

2. Bring water to a boil in a large pot. Blanch the green beans for 2 minutes, drain, and place the green beans in a bowl of ice water to stop the cooking.

3. Preheat the oven to 325°F and line a sheet pan with parchment paper or foil.

4. In a separate saucepan, melt the butter over medium heat, stirring constantly so the butter does not burn.

5. Add in the brown sugar and garlic powder. Stir until the sugar is fully dissolved.

6. Remove the saucepan from heat and stir in the soy sauce. Continue to stir as the mixture bubbles.

7. Toss the green beans in the sauce to fully coat.

8. Pour the green beans and the sauce onto the prepared sheet pan. Place in the oven and roast the green beans for 10 to 15 minutes.

9. Top with toasted sesame seeds before serving.

PREP TIME: 10 minutes | COOK TIME: 20-25 minutes

Pictured on page 92

SESAME CHICKEN STRIPS

{SERVES 4 TO 6}

These chicken strips are easy to make but pack a lot of flavor in each bite. The strips can be served for dinner, or you can choose to cut the chicken into smaller strips so they can be served as an appetizer. This is great for a gathering and the chicken strips can easily be kept in a warming drawer until served.

1. Preheat the oven to 425°F and prepare a rimmed sheet pan with a rack placed on top. Spray the pan and the rack with cooking spray.

2. In a medium mixing bowl, combine 1 cup mayonnaise, minced onion, and mustard.

3. In a separate bowl, combine the crushed crackers and sesame seeds.

4. Cut the chicken lengthwise into ¼-inch strips.

5. Dip each chicken strip into the mayonnaise mixture and then into the crushed cracker mixture to coat. Continue until all chicken strips are coated in the cracker crumbs.

6. Place the prepared chicken strips onto the rack in a single layer.

7. Place pan in oven and bake for 15 to 18 minutes, or until the juices run clear. Check that a thermometer inserted into the thickest chicken strip reads 165°F.

8. While the chicken strips are baking, combine the remaining 1 cup mayonnaise with the honey.

9. Serve the chicken strips immediately with the honey mayonnaise or my Honey Mustard (see below).

HONEY MUSTARD

1. Combine all ingredients in a small mixing bowl. Stir well to combine.

2. Serve with the sesame chicken strips and store any leftovers in an airtight container in the refrigerator.

PREP TIME: 25 minutes | BAKE TIME: 15-20 minutes

CHICKEN

Cooking spray

2 cups mayonnaise, divided

2 teaspoons minced Vidalia onion

2 teaspoons dried mustard

1 cup crushed Ritz® crackers

½ cup sesame seeds

2 pounds boneless, skinless chicken breasts

2 tablespoons honey

HONEY MUSTARD

½ cup mayonnaise

2 tablespoons honey

1 tablespoon Dijon-style mustard

1 tablespoon prepared yellow mustard

1 teaspoon apple cider vinegar

4 dashes Texas Pete® hot sauce

⅛ teaspoon kosher salt

⅛ teaspoon freshly ground black pepper

CHAPTER 3

Fall Gatherings

STUFFED FRENCH TOAST WITH APPLE CIDER SYRUP

{6 TO 8 SERVINGS;
SYRUP MAKES 1⅓ CUPS}

A great weekend breakfast treat to share with the family this fall. Go ahead and pick up some apple cider at the farmers market or the pumpkin patch to use for the syrup. It is the perfect addition to the stuffed French toast. This will be the new breakfast favorite!

---

1. Cut the French bread loaf into cubes. Prepare a 9 x 13-inch baking dish with cooking spray.

2. To assemble, place half of the bread cubes in the prepared baking dish. Top with the cream cheese cubes and then add the remaining bread cubes.

3. In a separate bowl, beat together the eggs, half-and-half, melted butter, and maple syrup until well combined.

4. Pour the egg mixture evenly over the bread and cream cheese cubes. Using a spatula, lightly press the layers down to moisten.

5. Cover the baking dish with plastic wrap and refrigerate for at least 2 hours, up to 24 hours.

6. When ready to serve, preheat the oven to 325°F.

7. Remove the plastic wrap and top with chopped pecans, if desired. Place the baking dish in the oven and bake for 35 to 40 minutes, or until the center is set and the edges are lightly golden brown.

8. Let stand for 10 minutes before serving. Top with the apple cider syrup or serve the syrup on the side.

APPLE CIDER SYRUP

1. In a small saucepan, stir together the sugar, cornstarch, and cinnamon. Once combined, stir in the apple cider and lemon juice.

2. Cook the mixture over medium heat, stirring often, until the mixture becomes thick and bubbly.

3. Once the mixture is thick, cook for another 2 minutes and then remove from heat.

4. Stir in the butter until melted.

NOTE: If you can't find apple cider, apple juice can be substituted.

FRENCH TOAST

1 (1-pound) loaf French bread, unsliced

Cooking spray

8 ounces cream cheese, cut into small cubes

8 large eggs

2½ cups half-and-half

⅓ cup unsalted butter, melted

¼ cup pure maple syrup

1 cup chopped pecans

APPLE CIDER SYRUP

½ cup granulated sugar

2 teaspoons cornstarch

½ teaspoon ground cinnamon

1 cup apple cider

1 tablespoon freshly squeezed lemon juice

2 tablespoons unsalted butter

PREP TIME: 20-30 minutes | BAKE TIME: 35-40 minutes

PUMPKIN NUT BREAD

{MAKES 1 (8 X 4-INCH) LOAF}

I love quick breads—this one, especially. My earliest marketing tools in catering were making breads for all the seasons. This one I always did around Halloween. The chopped pecans are optional but they add a great crunch to each slice.

Baking spray

1½ cups all-purpose flour

1¼ teaspoons baking soda

1 teaspoon kosher salt

1 teaspoon ground cinnamon

½ teaspoon ground nutmeg

1 cup granulated sugar

1 cup pumpkin puree

½ cup buttermilk, at room temperature

1 large egg, at room temperature

2 tablespoons unsalted butter, melted

½ cup chopped pecans, optional

1. Preheat the oven to 350°F and prepare an 8 x 4-inch loaf pan with baking spray.

2. In a large mixing bowl, sift together flour, baking soda, salt, and spices.

3. In another mixing bowl, combine the sugar, pumpkin, buttermilk, and egg. Mix well.

4. Pour the wet ingredient mixture into the dry ingredients. Beat well by hand until blended.

5. Stir in the melted butter and pecans.

6. Pour into the prepared loaf pan.

7. Bake for 1 hour, or until a toothpick inserted in the center comes out clean and the bread begins to pull away from the edges. Sometimes it needs an additional 5 minutes.

8. Let cool completely in the pan before transferring to a wire rack. Slice and enjoy.

PREP TIME: 15 minutes | BAKE TIME: 1 hour - 1 hour and 5 minutes

PECAN DUMP CAKE

{ S E R V E S   1 2   T O   1 8 }

The name of this recipe says it all! Truly just dump and layer all the ingredients together before throwing this cake in the oven. A great recipe for a block party or dinner with friends!

———

1. Preheat the oven to 325°F and prepare a 9 x 13-inch pan with baking spray.

2. In the bottom of the prepared pan, dump the cans of crushed pineapple and spread evenly. Do not drain.

3. Sprinkle the brown sugar over the pineapple.

4. Spread the yellow cake mix (unprepared) over the brown sugar and sprinkle the chopped pecans over the cake mix.

5. Pour the melted butter over the top of the nuts.

6. Bake for about 50 minutes, or until a toothpick inserted in the center of the cake comes out clean.

7. Remove from the oven and place the pan on a wire rack to cool. Let cool completely before slicing.

PREP TIME: 10 minutes | BAKE TIME: 50 minutes

Baking spray

2 (8-ounce) cans crushed pineapple in juice

1 cup firmly packed light brown sugar

1 (15.25-ounce) box yellow cake mix

1 cup chopped pecans

1 cup (2 sticks) unsalted butter, melted

PECAN STUFFED MUSHROOMS

{MAKES 15 TO 20 BITES}

This brings back memories of passing these on a beautiful silver tray in my early catering days. The reviews were always amazing.

———

Cooking spray

15 to 20 large button mushrooms

1 cup pecans, finely chopped

3 tablespoons minced fresh parsley

¼ cup (½ stick) unsalted butter, softened

1 clove garlic, minced

¼ teaspoon dried thyme

½ teaspoon kosher salt

Freshly ground black pepper, to taste

1. Preheat the oven to 350°F and prepare a shallow baking dish with cooking spray.
2. Clean the mushrooms. Slice off the stems and set the caps aside.
3. Finely chop the stems and place in a large bowl. Add in the pecans, parsley, butter, garlic, thyme, salt, and pepper. Mix well.
4. Place the caps in the prepared pan, hollow side up.
5. Stuff the caps with the pecan mixture.
6. Bake for 15 to 20 minutes. Serve immediately.

PREP TIME: 20-25 minutes | BAKE TIME: 15-20 minutes

CHEESE STRIPS

{MAKES 54 TO 72 STRIPS}

This is a great recipe to make on a rainy day! Make the recipe ahead of time and store the strips in the freezer. Bake them off when you need a great salad garnish or snack for cocktail hour.

———

1 loaf Pepperidge Farm® very thinly sliced white bread

8 ounces grated sharp cheddar cheese

6 slices crisp cooked bacon, crumbled

½ cup toasted slivered almonds

1 small Vidalia onion, finely chopped

1 cup Hellmann's® mayonnaise

Kosher salt, to taste

Freshly ground black pepper, to taste

1. Trim the crust from each slice of bread.
2. In a medium mixing bowl, combine the cheese, crumbled bacon, almonds, onion, mayonnaise, and salt and pepper to taste.
3. Spread a heaping tablespoon of the mixture onto each slice of bread. Cut each bread slice into 3 or 4 strips.
4. Place all prepared strips onto sheet pans covered with wax or parchment paper.
5. Place the pans in the freezer and freeze for at least an hour or two. Once frozen, they can be stored in a resealable plastic bag.
6. When ready to bake, preheat the oven to 400°F and place the frozen strips on a sheet pan.
7. Bake for approximately 10 minutes, or until the cheese has melted and is bubbly. Serve immediately.

PREP TIME: 20-25 minutes | BAKE TIME: 10 minutes

GERMAN SLAW

{ M A K E S 8 S E R V I N G S }

A different type of slaw to serve at the next fall party! I love the sweet and tangy sauce over the cabbage and sweet onion. Plan ahead so this slaw has plenty of time to chill in the refrigerator.

1. In a large bowl, place a layer of cabbage and then a layer of onion. Repeat until all the cabbage and onion is used.

2. In a heavy-bottomed saucepan set over medium heat, combine the sugar, white vinegar, salt, celery seed, and mustard. Stir and bring to a boil. Cook until all ingredients are well blended.

3. Reduce heat to medium-low and add in the oil. Stir well and heat.

4. Remove the pan from heat and pour the dressing over the cabbage mixture. Do not stir.

5. Cover the bowl and chill in the refrigerator. Let sit for 4 hours before serving.

6. Mix well when ready to serve.

PREP TIME: 30 minutes | CHILL TIME: 4 hours

1 large head cabbage, shredded

1 large Vidalia onion, sliced

¾ cup granulated sugar

1 cup white vinegar

1½ teaspoons kosher salt

1 teaspoon celery seed

1 teaspoon prepared yellow mustard

¾ cup vegetable oil

SPIDERS

{ 6 0   C O O K I E S }

Looking for a fun dessert to make with the children at the Halloween party? Look no further! This dessert is the perfect activity for the children, and they will love to be able to eat their creations later that night!

---

12 ounces butterscotch morsels

16 ounces semi-sweet chocolate morsels

4 cups salted peanuts

12 ounces chow mein noodles, uncooked

1. Microwave the butterscotch and chocolate morsels for 1 ½ minutes, stir. Return the bowl to the microwave and heat for another minute, stir. Place the dish back in the microwave and continue to heat in 30-second intervals until the chocolate mixture is smooth.

2. Add in the peanuts and chow mein noodles to the melted butterscotch mixture. Mix until everything is completely coated.

3. Line several baking sheets with parchment paper.

4. Place small half dollar-sized clusters on the prepared tray.

5. Refrigerate to harden for at least an hour.

SERVING SUGGESTION: These can be packaged in Halloween-themed cellophane bags as individual treats, or stored together in an airtight container.

PREP TIME: 15 minutes | CHILL TIME: At least 1 hour

ROASTED VEGETABLE LASAGNA

{ SERVES 10 TO 12 }

People are always looking for meatless dinner options; this is the perfect recipe for that. Roasting the vegetables for the lasagna adds so much more flavor, you won't even be missing the meat sauce! This was a Gourmet to Go favorite back at the Café and it is sure to be a guest favorite at your next gathering.

1. Preheat the oven to 400°F and prepare a 9 x 13-inch glass dish with cooking spray.

2. In a large mixing bowl, toss the sliced vegetables with the olive oil, kosher salt, black pepper, and minced garlic. Arrange on 2 medium sheet pans. (You can line the sheet pans with parchment paper or aluminum foil for easy clean-up.)

3. Place the sheet pans in the oven and bake for 15 to 20 minutes, or until tender and lightly browned.

4. Remove the roasted vegetables from the oven and place in a mixing bowl.

5. If you plan to bake the lasagna immediately, turn the oven down to 350°F.

6. Spoon ¼ (6 ounces) of the marinara sauce in the bottom of the prepared glass dish. Cover with a layer of 3 lasagna noodles.

7. Spread ½ of the ricotta over the noodles. Top with ½ of the vegetables, ⅓ of the mozzarella, ⅓ of the Parmesan, and then ¼ of the sauce. Repeat layering with the noodles, then the remaining ricotta and vegetables, ⅓ of the mozzarella, ⅓ of the Parmesan, and ¼ of the sauce. Add the final layer of noodles, the final ¼ of the sauce and the remaining mozzarella and Parmesan.

8. Bake for 25 to 30 minutes, or until the cheese is browned and the sauce is bubbling.

NOTE: If the lasagna is made ahead of time and refrigerated, bake for 30 to 35 minutes at 400°F. If frozen, let thaw overnight in the refrigerator and bake for 30 to 35 minutes at 400°F.

PREP TIME: 30 minutes | BAKE TIME: 40-50 minutes

Cooking spray

¾ pound zucchini, thinly sliced

¾ pound yellow squash, thinly sliced

1 large Vidalia onion, thinly sliced into half moons

1 small eggplant, thinly sliced

1 red bell pepper, thinly sliced into strips

1 yellow bell pepper, thinly sliced into strips

Extra-virgin olive oil, as needed

Kosher salt, to taste

Freshly ground black pepper, to taste

1 teaspoon minced garlic cloves

1 (24-ounce) jar marinara sauce, divided

9 lasagna noodles, cooked according to package directions

1½ cups ricotta cheese, divided

3⅓ cups shredded mozzarella cheese, divided

¾ cup shredded Parmesan cheese, divided

GHOST MERINGUES

{MAKES 3 DOZEN GHOSTS}

The perfect treat for the children at the Halloween party. They will fall in love with these ghosts! These meringue cookies also make great treats for your child's class party.

4 large egg whites

Pinch kosher salt

1 cup granulated sugar

1 teaspoon pure vanilla extract

Edible candy eyes (about 75)

Melted semi-sweet chocolate chips, as needed

1. Preheat the oven to 375°F and line sheet pans with parchment paper or aluminum foil.

2. In the bowl of a stand mixer, beat the egg whites and salt until soft peaks form.

3. Slowly add in the granulated sugar and continue to beat until stiff peaks form. Add in the vanilla extract until blended.

4. Fill a piping bag or resealable plastic bag with the meringue mixture. If using a piping bag, use a plain round piping tip. If using a resealable bag, cut the corner about ⅛ inch. Pipe the meringue into a 1 ½-inch circle; the base should come up to a central point to resemble a short ghost. Pipe each "ghost" about 2 inches apart on the sheet pans.

5. Place the pans in the oven, close the door, and turn off the oven. Let the meringues remain in the oven until the oven cools to room temperature, about 3 hours, or as long as overnight.

6. After cooling, place edible candy eyes on each ghost, using a small dollop of melted chocolate to hold the eyes in place.

PREP TIME: 5 minutes, plus assembly time
BAKE TIME: At least 3 hours

5 CHEESE BAKE

{MAKES 1 PAN; CUT INTO 9 SQUARES OR SMALLER}

I always prefer to buy blocks of cheese and shred or grate it myself. In my opinion, it tends to taste fresher this way. This is a great dish to share at the fall block party and one that everyone will enjoy.

———

1. Preheat the oven to 375°F and prepare a 9-inch square Pyrex® dish with cooking spray.

2. Place half of the crescent roll dough flat on the bottom of the prepared dish.

3. In a large bowl, mix together all of the cheeses and the beaten eggs. Add in the cream cheese and mix thoroughly.

4. Spoon the cheese mixture on top of the crescent roll dough.

5. Place the remaining crescent roll dough on top of the cheese mixture.

6. Pour the melted margarine over the top and sprinkle evenly with poppy seeds.

7. Place in the oven and bake for 30 minutes, or until the crescent roll dough is browned and cooked through.

8. Remove the pan from the oven and let cool slightly. Drizzle the honey over the top of the crescent dough, if desired.

9. Once cool enough to handle, cut into small squares.

Cooking spray

1 (8-ounce) can refrigerated crescent rolls, divided

¼ pound Monterey Jack cheese, grated

¼ pound sharp cheddar cheese, grated

¼ pound Muenster cheese, shredded

¼ pound Swiss cheese, grated

2 large eggs, beaten

8 ounces cream cheese, at room temperature

¼ cup (½ stick) margarine, melted

2 tablespoons poppy seeds, or more as needed

2 tablespoons honey, optional

PREP TIME: 20-25 minutes | BAKE TIME: 30 minutes

ARTICHOKE GRUYÈRE DIP

{1 (1½-QUART) CASSEROLE DISH}

Elevate your classic artichoke dip with both Asiago and Gruyère cheese. This recipe can easily be made ahead, an easy way to save time closer to the start of your event.

Cooking spray

2 cups shredded Parmesan cheese

½ cup shredded Asiago cheese

¼ cup shredded Gruyère cheese

2 teaspoons minced garlic

2½ cups Hellmann's® mayonnaise

7 ounces canned artichokes, quartered and roughly chopped

4 green onions, sliced

1 teaspoon kosher salt

¼ cup whole milk

½ cup heavy cream

½ cup plain bread crumbs

Crackers or pita chips, to serve

1. Preheat the oven to 375°F and prepare a 1½-quart casserole dish with cooking spray.

2. In a large bowl, mix together the Parmesan, Asiago, Gruyère, and garlic.

3. Add in the mayonnaise, artichokes, green onions, and salt. Slowly stir in the milk and heavy cream.

4. Transfer the mixture to the prepared casserole dish. Top with the bread crumbs, sprinkling evenly over the top.

5. Bake for 15 to 20 minutes, stirring gently halfway through.

6. Serve warm with crackers or pita chips.

To make ahead: Combine all ingredients for the dip and place in the prepared casserole dish. Do not top with the bread crumbs. Cover the casserole dish and place in the refrigerator until ready to bake. Thirty minutes before baking, let the dip come to room temperature and top with the bread crumbs. Continue with step 5.

PREP TIME: 25-30 minutes | BAKE TIME: 15-20 minutes

PUMPKIN CRISP

{SERVES 12 TO 18}

Melissa Carden was one of my commissary directors at the Café. She prepared this recipe when she invited her "boss" to dinner. I knew right away she was a keeper. This is a great dish to prepare with your children or grandchildren, as it comes together in one bowl!

1. Preheat the oven to 350°F and lightly grease a 9 x 13-inch pan with baking spray.

2. Stir together the pumpkin, milk, granulated sugar, and vanilla extract in a large mixing bowl.

3. Add in the cake mix and cinnamon. Stir well to combine.

4. Pour the batter into the prepared baking pan and sprinkle evenly with the chopped pecans and rolled oats. Drizzle the melted butter over the top.

5. Bake for 1 hour and 5 minutes.

6. Remove from the oven and let stand for 10 minutes before serving.

7. Serve warm or at room temperature with whipped cream or vanilla ice cream. Sprinkle ground nutmeg over the top.

PREP TIME: 15 minutes | BAKE TIME: 1 hour and 5 minutes

Pictured on page 124

Baking spray

1 (15-ounce) can pumpkin puree

1 cup evaporated milk

1 cup granulated sugar

1 teaspoon pure vanilla extract

1 (15.25-ounce) box butter-flavored yellow cake mix

½ teaspoon ground cinnamon

1 cup chopped pecans

1 cup old fashioned rolled oats

1 cup (2 sticks) unsalted butter, melted

Whipped cream, to garnish

Ground nutmeg, to garnish

APPLESAUCE CAKE

{1 (8X4-INCH) LOAF}

One of the easiest semi-homemade cakes to make. You may even have everything you need in your pantry! Be sure you purchase the unsweetened applesauce, otherwise the cake will be too sweet. Wrap any leftover cake in plastic wrap and store in the refrigerator.

———

1. Preheat the oven to 350°F and prepare a 10-inch loaf pan with baking spray. Wipe out any excess spray.

2. In a small bowl, mix together the cinnamon and granulated sugar.

3. Dust the inside of the greased loaf pan with 1 tablespoon of the cinnamon-sugar mixture.

4. In a mixing bowl, combine the cake mix, applesauce, and eggs with a wooden spoon until well blended.

5. Spread 2 cups of the batter in the loaf pan. Top evenly with the remaining cinnamon-sugar mixture. Take the remaining cake batter and spread evenly over the cinnamon-sugar.

6. Bake for 45 minutes, or until a toothpick inserted in the middle of the cake comes out clean.

7. Cool the cake in the pan for 15 minutes.

8. Transfer the cake to a wire rack, and let cool completely before serving.

NOTE: Any leftover cake should be refrigerated.

Baking spray

2 tablespoons ground cinnamon

¼ cup granulated sugar

1 (15.25-ounce) box yellow cake mix

1 ⅔ cups unsweetened applesauce

3 large eggs, at room temperature

PREP TIME: 10-12 minutes | BAKE TIME: 45 minutes

BUFFALO CHICKEN DIP

{MAKES 7 CUPS}

I don't think this recipe needs a lot of explaining. It is truly a fan favorite! Bring this dish to the tailgate and they might even name you the MVP.

---

4 to 5 boneless, skinless chicken breasts

Cooking spray

16 ounces cream cheese

1 (1-ounce) package dry ranch seasoning

6 tablespoons Frank's® Red Hot Buffalo wing sauce

½ cup shredded cheddar cheese

Crackers or fresh vegetables, for serving

1. Place the chicken breasts in a large pot with water set over medium-high heat. Bring it to a boil and boil the chicken until a thermometer inserted in the middle of a chicken breast reads 165°F or higher. Test to see if the chicken is ready by pushing a fork into it and seeing if it can be easily shredded.

2. Once ready, turn off the burner and remove the chicken from the boiling water. Place on a cutting board to cool slightly. When the chicken is cool enough to handle, shred by hand with two forks or place the chicken in the bowl of a stand mixer. Using the paddle attachment, turn the mixer on low or medium speed to shred the chicken.

3. Preheat the oven to 350°F and prepare a large casserole dish with cooking spray.

4. In a microwave-safe bowl, place the cream cheese in the microwave and melt slightly until softened and easy to mix.

5. Stir in the ranch seasoning packet and Buffalo sauce. Mix until fully combined.

6. In the prepared casserole dish, mix together the shredded chicken and the cream cheese mixture.

7. Top with the cheddar cheese and place in the oven. Bake for about 20 minutes, or until the cheese is melted.

8. Serve warm with your favorite crackers and vegetables.

PREP TIME: 20 minutes | BAKE TIME: 20 minutes

HOT DOG CHILI

{SERVES 8 TO 10}

Chili is a fantastic tailgating recipe that can easily be kept warm in a slow cooker. This chili is on the thicker side so it makes a wonderful topping on a hot dog, but it can just as easily be enjoyed on its own.

1. Heat the oil in a large Dutch oven set over medium heat. Add in the ground beef, ground pork, minced garlic, and diced onion.

2. Brown the meat, using a wooden spoon to break it up into little pieces. Cook until the meat is browned throughout.

3. Add in Worcestershire, hot sauce, and all the seasonings and spices. Stir to combine.

4. Add in the can of chili beans, ketchup, mustard, water, and tomato sauce. Stir to combine and reduce heat to low.

5. Simmer the chili for at least 30 minutes, until thickened.

6. Serve hot over hot dogs or on its own with desired toppings such as cheese, green onions, sour cream, or chips.

PREP TIME: 15 minutes | COOK TIME: 45 minutes

1 tablespoon vegetable oil

1½ pounds ground beef (80/20)

1 pound ground pork

2 teaspoons minced garlic

1 small Vidalia onion, diced

2 tablespoons Worcestershire sauce

1 tablespoon hot sauce

2 tablespoons plus 2 teaspoons chili powder

1 teaspoon dry mustard

1 teaspoon onion powder

1½ teaspoons cumin

1 (16-ounce) can mild chili beans

1½ cups ketchup

½ cup prepared yellow mustard

3 tablespoons water

3 tablespoons tomato sauce

TOPPINGS

Shredded cheddar cheese

Chopped green onions

Sour cream

Fritos® or tortilla chips

THE PERFECT HOT DOG—TWO WAYS

Slice a hot dog down the middle vertically and either grill or pan-fry it. It gives a wonderful crisp to the hot dog and since it is sliced, it makes the perfect vehicle for the chili!

If you would prefer to boil the hot dogs, boil them in beer. Using 12 ounces of beer (I prefer to use a lager), bring beer to a boil in a medium saucepan. Poke the hot dogs with a fork several times. Place the hot dogs in the boiling beer and boil for 5 minutes, or until heated through. An alternative to boiling would be to slowly simmer the hot dogs in the beer. This will allow more time for the hot dogs to soak up the flavor. Either way, you can't go wrong!

CONFETTI PASTA SALAD

{ SERVES 4 TO 6 }

PASTA SALAD

8 ounces uncooked small shell pasta

1 pint container grape tomatoes, halved

2 cups coarsely chopped fresh spinach

1 yellow bell pepper, chopped

¼ cup finely chopped red onion

3 tablespoons chopped fresh dill

1 (4-ounce) container crumbled feta cheese

VINAIGRETTE

¼ cup freshly squeezed lemon juice (1 medium lemon)

1 teaspoon Dijon-style mustard

1 large garlic clove, minced

¼ teaspoon kosher salt

¼ teaspoon freshly ground black pepper

½ cup vegetable oil

A delicious and colorful pasta salad for the tailgating table. Slightly different from the classic pasta salad, with fresh dill and feta cheese, it will definitely become a staple for every tailgate. When mixing the vinaigrette with the pasta and vegetables, start with half and save some of the remaining vinaigrette to mix in right before serving.

1. Cook the pasta according to package directions. Drain and set aside to cool.

2. Combine the prepared vegetables and dill in a large mixing bowl.

3. For the vinaigrette, combine the lemon juice, mustard, garlic, kosher salt, and black pepper in a small mixing bowl. Slowly whisk in the oil until combined.

4. Toss pasta with mixed vegetables and the vinaigrette. Add in the crumbled feta and mix until the pasta salad is thoroughly combined.

5. Serve immediately, or cover and chill for up to 8 hours.

PREP TIME: 20-25 minutes | CHILL TIME: Up to 8 hours

Pictured on page 144

SPICY OATMEAL RAISIN BARS
{MAKES 1 HALF SHEET PAN, 40 SQUARES}

The oatmeal cookie's older and more sophisticated brother. So much flavor packed in one bar! These bars can also be made ahead of time and frozen until needed. You can choose to freeze the entire pan or go ahead and slice the bars and freeze them individually.

---

1. Preheat the oven to 350°F and prepare a 13 x 18-inch rimmed sheet pan with baking spray.

2. In the bowl of a stand mixer, combine the brown sugar, granulated sugar, and butter. Mix on medium speed for 3 to 4 minutes, or until light and fluffy.

3. Add in the eggs and vanilla extract. Beat at medium speed, scraping the bowl often, until combined.

4. Add in the oats, flour, baking soda, and spices. Beat at low speed, scraping the bowl as needed. Mix until fully combined.

5. By hand, stir in the coconut, raisins or dried cranberries, pecans, and chocolate morsels.

6. Spread the oat mixture in the prepared pan and bake for 25 minutes, or until browned and cooked through.

7. Remove from the oven and let cool completely on a wire rack before cutting into bars.

Baking spray

½ cup firmly packed light brown sugar

½ cup granulated sugar

1 cup (2 sticks) unsalted butter, at room temperature

2 large eggs, at room temperature

2 teaspoons pure vanilla extract

1 ½ cups rolled oats

1 cup all-purpose flour

1 teaspoon baking soda

1 teaspoon ground cinnamon

½ teaspoon kosher salt

½ teaspoon ground ginger

¼ teaspoon ground nutmeg

1 cup shredded sweetened coconut

1 cup raisins or dried cranberries

½ cup chopped pecans

1 cup semi-sweet chocolate morsels

PREP TIME: 20-25 minutes | BAKE TIME: 25 minutes

Pictured on page 149

KAHLÚA® BROWNIES

{MAKES 1 HALF SHEET PAN (13 X 18 INCHES), 40 SQUARES}

Brownies kicked up with both Kahlúa® and a beautiful cream cheese swirl! The Kahlúa® in these brownies not only adds extra flavor but also helps keep the brownies super moist. The cream cheese swirl on top will definitely catch everyone's attention at the tailgate!

DROP BATTER

Baking spray

4 ounces cream cheese, at room temperature

3 tablespoons unsalted butter, at room temperature

⅓ cup granulated sugar

1 large egg, at room temperature

2 ½ tablespoons self-rising flour

BROWNIE BATTER

3 ¾ cups granulated sugar

2 ⅔ cups all-purpose flour

1 ½ cups dark cocoa powder

¾ teaspoon baking powder

¾ teaspoon kosher salt

¾ cup (1 ½ sticks) unsalted butter, cut into small cubes and softened

1 ½ cups Kahlúa® Rum and Coffee Liqueur

6 large eggs, at room temperature

1. Preheat the oven to 325°F and prepare a rimmed sheet pan with baking spray.

2. In the bowl of a stand mixer fitted with the paddle attachment, beat the cream cheese, butter, and sugar on medium speed, until creamy, about 3 minutes. Add in the egg and beat well. Scrape the sides of the bowl, add in the flour, and beat until well blended. Transfer the drop batter to another bowl and set aside.

3. Clean the bowl of the stand mixer and start on the brownie mixture. In the bowl, mix together the sugar, flour, cocoa, baking powder, and salt.

4. Stir in the butter pieces and Kahlúa®. Beat with the paddle attachment on medium speed until smooth.

5. Beat in the 6 eggs, one at a time. Mix until smooth and scrape the sides of the bowl.

6. Transfer the mixture to the prepared baking pan, spreading evenly.

7. Spoon the cheese mixture over the chocolate batter, spacing evenly. Run a knife through the batter to swirl.

8. Place in the oven and bake for 35 minutes. After baking, remove from the oven and cool completely on a wire rack before cutting.

9. Cut into bars and enjoy!

PREP TIME: 20 minutes | BAKE TIME: 35 minutes

SAUSAGE CHEESE BALLS

{MAKES 60 TO 70}

A Southern classic that can be eaten any time of day. Serve these poppable bites warm or even at room temperature. If desired, these can be served with honey mustard or maple syrup.

———

1. Preheat the oven to 350°F and line 2 sheet pans with parchment paper.

2. Pour the baking mix into a large bowl. Add in the sausage, grated cheese, and water.

3. Mix well by hand until the mixture comes together in a ball.

4. Roll into 1¼-inch balls (slightly bigger than a quarter) and place on the prepared sheet pans.

5. Bake for 15 minutes, or until browned on the bottom.

NOTE: Serve the sausage balls skewered between two thin slices of raw radish for a delicious appetizer!

PREP TIME: 10-15 minutes | BAKE TIME: 15 minutes

1 (5.5-ounce) package
Bisquick® baking mix
(1⅓ cups)

1 pound Jimmy Dean®
Hot ground sausage

8 ounces Cracker Barrel®
sharp cheddar cheese, grated

3 tablespoons water

PECAN ORANGE MUFFINS
{ MAKES 12 MUFFINS }

These muffins are perfectly moist and sweet. This is a great breakfast snack for setting up the tailgate in the morning, or for the noon games when the tailgating starts earlier than normal! It may seem different to pour the orange juice on top of the muffin batter but it all bakes into the muffin.

Baking spray

½ cup (1 stick) unsalted butter, softened

1 cup granulated sugar

2 large eggs, at room temperature

1 teaspoon baking soda

2 cups all-purpose flour

1 cup plain yogurt or buttermilk

¾ cup finely chopped pecans

Freshly grated peel of 1 orange

⅓ cup freshly squeezed orange juice

2 tablespoons turbinado sugar

1. Preheat the oven to 375°F and prepare a muffin pan with baking spray.

2. In the bowl of a stand mixer, beat the butter and granulated sugar until pale yellow and creamy. Scrape the bowl as needed.

3. Add the eggs, one at a time, beating well after each addition.

4. Add in the baking soda and beat until combined. Remove the mixing bowl from the stand mixer and continue the rest of the recipe by hand.

5. Fold in half of the flour with a rubber spatula, and then half of the yogurt or buttermilk. Repeat the process with the remaining flour and liquid. Only mix until just combined, do not overmix!

6. Fold in the pecans and grated orange peel.

7. Spoon the batter into the prepared muffin cups. Pour the orange juice over the top of each muffin cup filled with batter (about one teaspoon over each cup).

8. Sprinkle the 2 tablespoons of turbinado sugar over the top of the muffin batter.

9. Bake for 25 to 27 minutes, or until a toothpick inserted in the center of the muffin comes out clean.

10. Remove from the oven and let the muffins cool slightly in the pan. When cool enough to handle, remove the muffins from the muffin pan and let them cool completely on a wire rack.

PREP TIME: 25 minutes | BAKE TIME: 25-27 minutes

HAM & POPPY SEED SLIDERS

{MAKES 12 SLIDERS}

Another classic appetizer with my own twist. Instead of only using yellow mustard in the sauce, I also like to add in some Durkee® sauce. Durkee® is a mayonnaise-mustard mixture that just adds a little something extra to this recipe.

Cooking spray

½ cup (1 stick) unsalted butter, melted

2 tablespoons grated Vidalia onion

2 teaspoons Worcestershire sauce

2 teaspoons poppy seeds

1 tablespoon light brown sugar

1 teaspoon Durkee sauce®

1 teaspoon prepared yellow mustard

1 (12-count) package sweet Hawaiian rolls

½ pound thinly sliced ham

6 slices Swiss cheese

1. Preheat the oven to 350°F and prepare a 9 x 13-inch baking dish with cooking spray.

2. In a mixing bowl, combine the melted butter, grated onion, Worcestershire, poppy seeds, brown sugar, Durkee® sauce, and yellow mustard. Stir until well mixed.

3. Remove the dinner rolls from the package and split the rolls in half. I use a long, serrated knife to slice through the entire package of rolls, splitting them in half without separating into individual rolls. Place the bottom half of the rolls in the prepared baking dish, cut-side up.

4. Spread half of the butter mixture on the bottom half of the rolls.

5. Layer the sliced ham and sliced cheese on top. Cover with the top half of the Hawaiian rolls.

6. Pour the remaining butter mixture on top of the rolls and brush to spread.

7. Cover with foil and bake for 15 minutes. Remove the pan from the oven and remove the foil. Return the pan to the oven and bake for 5 more minutes.

8. Let the rolls cool slightly before separating and serving.

PREP TIME: 20-25 minutes | BAKE TIME: 20 minutes

BARBECUED SAUSAGES

{MAKES 70 MINI SAUSAGES}

The perfect bite for a tailgating appetizer. These little sausages are so easy to snack on and travel great to any destination. To keep the sausages warm, either use a slow cooker or wrap the casserole dish in foil and place in a cooler without ice.

Cooking spray

1 tablespoon packed light brown sugar

1½ cups ketchup

¼ cup red wine vinegar

1 teaspoon Tabasco® hot sauce

1 teaspoon Worcestershire sauce

1 teaspoon prepared yellow mustard

1 clove garlic, minced

Kosher salt, to taste

Freshly ground black pepper, to taste

2 (12-ounce) packages, Hillshire Farm® Beef Lit'l Smokies

1. Preheat the oven to 350°F and prepare a small casserole dish with cooking spray.

2. In a mixing bowl, combine the sugar, ketchup, vinegar, hot sauce, Worcestershire, mustard, and garlic. Mix thoroughly.

3. Add in the sausages, salt and pepper to taste, and toss until the pieces are fully covered. Pour the sausages and sauce into the prepared casserole dish.

4. Bake for 1 hour, until the sausages are hot and the sauce is bubbly.

*This can also be done in a slow cooker set on low for 1 to 2 hours. When ready to serve, set the slow cooker to "keep warm."

PREP TIME: 10-15 minutes | BAKE TIME: 1 hour

Pictured on page 155

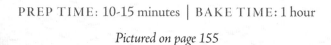

SEC PINWHEELS
{MAKES 30 TO 36}

The Southern twist on a classic pinwheel that is equally refreshing and hearty. An easy fan favorite for the next tailgate, this snack can be made ahead and can feed a crowd. You can always choose to swap out the meats and cheeses to make different varieties. Having your ingredients prepped and set out on your counter will make rolling the tortillas go by much faster!

4 ounces cream cheese, at room temperature

1 tablespoon prepared horseradish

½ teaspoon freshly ground black pepper

6 (8-inch) flour tortillas

12 slices provolone or Swiss cheese, thinly sliced

12 thin slices oven-roasted turkey

6 thin slices ham

18 slices cooked thick-cut bacon

1 medium English cucumber, peeled, thinly sliced, and water wrung

3 radishes, thinly sliced

1. In a small mixing bowl, add the cream cheese, horseradish, and black pepper. Mix together until thoroughly incorporated.

2. Spread a thin layer of the cream cheese mixture on each flour tortilla.

3. Top each tortilla with 2 slices of provolone or Swiss cheese, 2 slices of turkey, 1 slice of ham, and 3 slices of bacon.

4. Top each tortilla evenly with the cucumbers and radish slices.

5. Tightly roll up the tortilla; wrap it in wax paper to hold it together.

6. Repeat until all tortillas are rolled up and wrapped.

7. Place wrapped tortillas in the refrigerator for a few hours or overnight.

8. When ready to serve, cut off ends, then cut into 1-inch slices. These can be plated on a platter with a toothpick in each slice for easy pick-up.

PREP TIME: 20 minutes

Pictured on page 155

MASHED POTATOES
AND GRAVY

CHICKEN AND BACON CHOWDER

{SERVES 6}

Everyone knows how busy the days surrounding Thanksgiving can be and this is the perfect soup to make on one of those nights. This soup can easily be made into a meal with a simple salad on the side.

---

4 slices thick-cut bacon, chopped

3 stalks celery, finely chopped

2 medium shallots, finely chopped

¼ teaspoon cayenne pepper

¾ teaspoon kosher salt, divided

½ cup all-purpose flour

4 cups low-sodium chicken broth

1 pound skinless, boneless chicken thighs

1 pound red potatoes, cut into ½-inch chunks

2 cups whole milk

2 cups fresh or frozen corn

Thinly sliced basil, for garnish

Oyster crackers, for serving

1. In a 6-quart pot over medium heat, cook the bacon until crispy and browned, stirring occasionally.

2. Using a slotted spoon, transfer the bacon pieces to a paper towel-lined plate and set aside.

3. To the pot, add the celery, shallots, cayenne, and ¼ teaspoon kosher salt. Cook for 7 to 10 minutes, or until the vegetables are almost tender, stirring occasionally.

4. Sprinkle the flour over the vegetables and cook for 1 minute, stirring constantly.

5. Slowly stir in the broth. Bring the soup to a simmer over high heat.

6. Add in the chicken and potatoes. Reduce the heat to medium and cook for 12 to 15 minutes, or until the chicken is cooked through and the potatoes are tender, stirring occasionally. A thermometer inserted in the thickest piece of chicken should read 165°F.

7. Using tongs, transfer the chicken to a bowl and shred by hand with two forks. Return the shredded chicken to the pot.

8. Stir in the milk, corn, and the remaining ½ teaspoon kosher salt. Cook for 3 minutes, or until the corn is hot.

9. Remove from heat and garnish the soup with basil and reserved bacon pieces. Serve with oyster crackers, if desired.

PREP TIME: 15 minutes | COOK TIME: 30 minutes

BAKED CHEESE GRITS
{MAKES 8 SERVINGS}

These baked cheese grits are perfect for a special Thanksgiving day breakfast alongside a quiche. Once the grits are cooking in the oven, you will have time to go ahead and start working on prep for Thanksgiving dinner. My favorite is always Cracker Barrel® cheese, but no matter which brand, make sure you use sharp cheddar cheese so the stronger cheddar flavor comes through.

———

1. Preheat the oven to 350°F and prepare a 3-quart casserole dish with cooking spray.

2. Combine the water and salt in a large pot; bring to a boil.

3. Stir in the grits, whisking constantly. Follow the package directions for how long to cook the grits.

4. Remove from heat and add in the butter and 3 ¾ cups grated cheese. Stir until the butter and cheese have melted into the grits.

5. Pour a small amount of the grits into the bowl with the beaten eggs to temper the eggs. Then stir the egg mixture into the pan with the remaining grits.

6. Pour the grits into the prepared casserole dish and sprinkle with the remaining ¼ cup of shredded cheese.

7. Bake for 1 hour and 15 minutes. Serve immediately. Store any leftovers in an airtight container in the refrigerator.

PREP TIME: 30 minutes | BAKE TIME: 1 hour 15 minutes

Cooking spray

6 cups water

2½ teaspoons kosher salt

1½ cups uncooked stone ground grits

½ cup (1 stick) unsalted butter

4 cups grated Cracker Barrel® sharp cheddar cheese, divided

3 large eggs, beaten

BITSY'S SPANKIN' VEGETABLE BEEF SOUP

{SERVES 10 TO 12}

6 to 8 pounds cross-cut beef shanks or hind shanks

4 teaspoons kosher salt, divided

10 cups beef broth

3 stalks celery, chopped

3 large carrots, peeled and chopped

2 medium Vidalia onions, chopped

1 (28-ounce) can crushed tomatoes

1 (14.5-ounce) can diced tomatoes

½ cup chopped fresh flat-leaf parsley

1 teaspoon dried basil

1 teaspoon dried thyme

½ teaspoon freshly ground black pepper

1 (6-ounce) can tomato paste

2 teaspoons Worcestershire sauce

1 (12-ounce) package frozen baby lima beans

1 (10-ounce) package frozen corn

1 (10-ounce) package frozen peas

1 (12-ounce) package frozen okra

½ cup pearl barley

2 (15-ounce) cans tomato sauce

1 teaspoon Montreal Steak® seasoning

This is my sister's recipe and one I love to make for a large crowd. It is a hearty soup that can be served for lunch or dinner! Be sure to freeze any leftovers, as the extra soup would be great to pull out and defrost for a rainy day.

1. In a large pot set over high heat add the beef shanks, 2 teaspoons salt, and the beef broth. Bring to a boil.

2. Add in the celery, carrots, onions, crushed tomatoes, diced tomatoes, parsley, basil, thyme, black pepper, tomato paste, and Worcestershire sauce. Simmer over low heat, uncovered, for 2 hours.

3. After 2 hours, remove the meat from the pot and chop it up. Return the meat to the pot.

4. Keeping heat on high, add in the remaining 2 teaspoons salt, all frozen vegetables, barley, tomato sauce, and Montreal seasoning.

5. Bring to a boil, then reduce the heat to low. Simmer for at least one hour longer.

6. Serve hot and enjoy! Any leftovers can be frozen in an airtight container.

PREP TIME: 1 hour | COOK TIME: 3 hours

BROCCOLI CREAM SAUCE

{MAKES 4 TO 6 SERVINGS}

This is a great sauce to take your broccoli up a notch! If you are looking for a different side dish for Thanksgiving, try the Broccoli Elegant.

---

1. Melt the butter in a heavy-bottomed saucepan set over low heat. Add in the flour, stirring constantly until smooth. Cook for 1 minute.

2. Stir in the bouillon and gradually add in the milk. Cook over medium heat until thick and bubbly.

3. Add in the cream cheese and salt, stirring until smooth. Stir in the sliced green onions and season with pepper.

4. Spoon over steamed or roasted broccoli, as needed. Any leftover sauce can be refrigerated up to 1 week.

NOTE: Another great way to serve broccoli with cream sauce is the Broccoli Elegant. Using my Southern Sage and Cornbread Dressing from my first cookbook, *The VeryVera Cookbook: Recipes from My Table*, spoon the dressing around the edges of a 9 x 13-inch dish. If you do not have time to make homemade dressing, my go-to is the Pepperidge Farm® stuffing mix. Place steamed or blanched broccoli in the middle of the dish and pour the cream sauce over the top of the broccoli. Cover the dish with aluminum foil and place in a 350°F oven. Bake for 20 to 25 minutes, or until heated through. Remove the aluminum foil and sprinkle with grated Parmesan or Cheddar cheese.

2 tablespoons unsalted butter

2 tablespoons all-purpose flour

1 tablespoon Better Than Bouillon® Roasted Chicken Base

¾ cup whole milk

3 ounces cream cheese

¼ teaspoon kosher salt

4 green onions, thinly sliced

Freshly ground black pepper, to taste

16 to 20 ounces steamed or roasted broccoli

PREP TIME: 5 minutes | COOK TIME: 10-15 minutes

HOLIDAY BAKED FRUIT
{SERVES 8}

A sweet side dish! This classically Southern dish will warm you from the inside out. Choose a mix of your favorite fruits to use for this dish. Most people choose to use canned fruit when making this dish, but I always prefer to use fresh fruit when possible.

Cooking spray

16 coconut macaroon cookies, crumbled

4 cups fruit (fresh peaches, fresh pears, fresh pineapple chunks, Cosmic Crisp® apples, blackberries)

¾ cup pecan halves, toasted

¼ cup firmly packed light brown sugar

½ cup golden sherry

¼ cup (½ stick) unsalted butter, melted

1. Preheat the oven to 350°F and prepare a 2½-quart baking dish with cooking spray.

2. In the prepared baking dish, layer ¼ of the crumbled cookies, ⅓ the fruit, and ¼ cup pecans.

3. Repeat all layers twice more. Top with the brown sugar and the remaining cookie crumbs.

4. Combine the sherry and melted butter in a small mixing bowl. Pour over the layered ingredients in the baking dish.

5. Bake uncovered for 30 minutes, or until heated through.

*If prepared ahead of time, do not pour the sherry mixture until just prior to baking.

PREP TIME: 15 minutes | BAKE TIME: 30 minutes

GERMAN CHOCOLATE PIE

{SERVES 8 TO 10}

Anyone who has read through my first cookbook knows that my birthday cake is always a German chocolate cake. So of course I love to have a German chocolate pie at Thanksgiving! Not your traditional choice but definitely a delicious one.

———

1. Preheat the oven to 400°F and place the pie crust in a 9-inch pie dish. Crimp the edges if desired and prick the bottom and sides with a fork.

2. In a large mixing bowl, combine the sugar, flour, cornstarch, cocoa powder, and salt.

3. In a blender, add the eggs, melted butter, milk, and vanilla. Add in the coconut and chopped pecans. Pulse briefly to combine.

4. Add the dry ingredients to the blender and pulse to combine.

5. Pour the entire mixture into the prepared pie crust.

6. Place in the oven and bake for 30 minutes.

7. Remove from the oven and allow to cool completely before slicing. Serve with whipped cream.

PREP TIME: 25 minutes | BAKE TIME: 30 minutes

---

1 Pillsbury® refrigerated pie crust, unbaked

1 cup granulated sugar

2 tablespoons all-purpose flour

1 tablespoon cornstarch

2 tablespoons Hershey's® unsweetened cocoa powder, sifted

Pinch of kosher salt

2 large eggs, at room temperature

3 tablespoons unsalted butter, melted

⅔ cup whole milk, at room temperature

1 teaspoon pure vanilla extract

¾ cup shredded coconut

½ cup pecans, roughly chopped

Whipped cream, for topping

PECAN PIE
{SERVES 6 TO 8}

Truly the most classic Thanksgiving dessert. Placing the pecans neatly and uniformly at the bottom of the pie crust will create a beautiful presentation when the pie is baked. This recipe can easily be prepared the day before in order to save time the day of Thanksgiving.

1 Pillsbury® refrigerated pie crust, unbaked

1 cup pecan halves

3 large eggs, lightly beaten

1 cup light corn syrup

1 cup firmly packed light brown sugar

⅓ cup unsalted butter, melted

⅛ teaspoon kosher salt

1 teaspoon pure vanilla extract

Ice cream or whipped cream, for topping

1. Preheat the oven to 350°F.

2. Press the unbaked pie crust into the bottom and sides of a 9-inch pie dish. Crimp the crust, if desired, and place the pecan halves flat-side down in the bottom of the crust.

3. In a mixing bowl, add the eggs, corn syrup, brown sugar, melted butter, salt, and vanilla. Stir by hand until well blended.

4. Pour the egg mixture into the pie crust over the pecans. The pecans will float to the top.

5. Bake for 25 to 30 minutes, then cover the edges of pie crust with foil to prevent overbrowning. Continue cooking an additional 30 minutes until the crust is lightly browned and filling is puffy.

6. Let the pie cool to room temperature before cutting and serving.

7. Serve with ice cream or top with whipped cream.

PREP TIME: 20 minutes | BAKE TIME: 55-60 minutes

RAISIN SAUCE
{MAKES 1½ CUPS}

If you're looking for a quick dinner the week of Thanksgiving, add this raisin sauce to the rotation. This is a perfect sauce for ham steak or pork, and this meal will put you in the holiday mood.

———

1 cup raisins

1¾ cups water

⅓ cup firmly packed light brown sugar

1½ teaspoons cornstarch

¼ teaspoon kosher salt

¼ teaspoon ground cinnamon

¼ teaspoon ground cloves

¼ teaspoon dry mustard

1 tablespoon distilled white vinegar

1. Add the raisins and water to a medium saucepan. Bring to a boil for 5 minutes.

2. In a small mixing bowl, combine the brown sugar, cornstarch, salt, and spices. Add the sugar mixture into the saucepan with the raisins. Cook, stirring until thickened, for about 5 minutes more.

3. Pour in the vinegar and stir until combined.

4. Serve warm with a ham steak or pork. (I love it with thin, fried chops!)

PREP TIME: 10 minutes | COOK TIME: 10-15 minutes

PECAN SQUARES
{MAKES 1 HALF SHEET PAN}

A great alternative to pecan pie if you need to serve a large crowd—or need a dessert for the holiday potluck. A delicious bite that doesn't skimp on the flavor!

1. Preheat the oven to 350°F and prepare a 13 x 18 rimmed sheet pan with baking spray.

2. Beat the butter and granulated sugar in the bowl of a stand mixer fitted with a paddle attachment, until light and fluffy, about 3 minutes.

3. Add the eggs and vanilla extract and mix well.

4. In a separate bowl, sift together the flour, baking powder, and salt. Mix the dry ingredients into the batter with the mixer on low speed until just combined.

5. The dough will be very sticky; sprinkle the dough and your hands lightly with flour.

6. Press the dough into the half sheet pan, making an edge around the outside.

7. Bake for 15 minutes, or until the crust is set but not browned. Allow to cool completely.

8. While crust is cooling, combine the butter, honey, brown sugar, and grated lemon peel in a heavy-bottomed saucepan.

9. Cook over low heat until the butter is melted, using a wooden spoon to stir.

10. Raise the heat and boil for 3 minutes, then remove from heat.

11. Stir in the heavy cream and pecans and pour the mixture over the crust.

12. Bake for 25 to 30 minutes, or until the filling is set. Remove from the oven and let cool completely. Once cooled, wrap in plastic wrap and refrigerate until cold.

13. Cut into bars and enjoy!

PREP TIME: 25-30 minutes | BAKE TIME: 40-45 minutes

CRUST

Baking spray

1 cup (2 sticks) unsalted butter, at room temperature

⅓ cup granulated sugar

2 large eggs, at room temperature

¼ teaspoon pure vanilla extract

2¼ cups all-purpose flour, plus extra for dusting

¼ teaspoon baking powder

⅛ teaspoon kosher salt

PECAN FILLING

1 cup (2 sticks) unsalted butter

½ cup pure honey

1½ cups firmly packed light brown sugar

½ teaspoon freshly grated lemon peel

2 tablespoons heavy cream

4 cups pecans, coarsely chopped

TOLLHOUSE PANCAKES WITH CREAMY TURKEY FILLING

{SERVES 6 TO 8}

The original recipe uses chicken, but leftover turkey would be great! This is a fun and different way to serve turkey and the kids will be so excited that they get pancakes for dinner! I prefer to use dark meat in mine, but it works well with both.

TURKEY FILLING AND MUSHROOM SAUCE

6 tablespoons unsalted butter

⅓ cup all-purpose flour

1 teaspoon kosher salt

2⅔ cups turkey broth (chicken broth can be substituted)

2 cups cooked turkey, shredded

⅔ cup sliced button mushrooms

⅓ cup half-and-half

TOLLHOUSE PANCAKES

4 large eggs, separated

2½ cups buttermilk

1 teaspoon baking soda

2 cups all-purpose flour

1 tablespoon plus 1 teaspoon granulated sugar

2 teaspoons baking powder

½ teaspoon kosher salt

4 tablespoons salted butter, at room temperature

Vegetable oil or shortening for preparing the griddle

4 tablespoons grated Parmesan cheese

1. Melt the butter in a saucepan set over medium heat.

2. Stir in the flour and salt until combined.

3. Gradually add in the broth, stirring constantly until thick. Divide this sauce in half by pouring half into a new saucepan.

4. In the original saucepan, add in the turkey, and heat thoroughly. Set aside or leave on low heat to keep warm until ready to use.

5. In the new saucepan, make the mushroom sauce by stirring in the sliced mushrooms and half-and-half. Keep warm in the saucepan over low heat until ready to use.

6. In the bowl of a stand mixer, with whisk attachment, beat egg whites until stiff peaks form. Transfer to another bowl.

7. Clean the mixing bowl and add in buttermilk, egg yolks, and baking soda and mix until combined.

8. Sift together the flour, sugar, baking powder, and salt and add to the mixing bowl and blend on low speed. Add in the butter and beat until smooth. Remove the bowl from the mixer.

9. Fold in the egg whites by hand, be careful not to deflate the batter.

10. Prepare the griddle with vegetable oil or shortening and set to medium heat.

11. Drop ⅓ cup of the pancake batter at a time onto the hot griddle, making about 5-inch pancakes.

12. When the cakes begin to bubble and the edges are cooked, flip the pancakes, and continue to cook on the other side.

13. When the pancakes are done, remove from the griddle and place on a plate until all the pancakes are cooked.

14. Turn the oven on to broil.

15. Add a heaping tablespoon of turkey filling on each pancake and roll up like a jelly roll. Place the rolled pancakes in a glass casserole dish.

16. Top with the mushroom sauce and sprinkle with Parmesan cheese. Broil until golden and serve immediately!

PREP TIME: 15 minutes | COOK TIME: 20 minutes

CHAPTER 4

Winter Socials

CHICKEN TETRAZZINI
{SERVES 6 TO 8}

A classic recipe everyone will enjoy. I love how quickly this recipe comes together. The secret is the use of Velveeta® cheese…it melts perfectly and helps make this dish so creamy. Hope your family enjoys it as much as mine does!

Cooking spray

1 teaspoon Better Than Bouillon® Roasted Chicken base

8 ounces bucatini pasta

5 tablespoons unsalted butter

¼ cup chopped Vidalia onion

½ pound fresh baby bella mushrooms, sliced (optional)

¼ cup all-purpose flour

2 cups chicken broth

¼ to ½ cup half-and-half

8 ounces Velveeta® cheese, cut into chunks

2 teaspoons kosher salt

⅛ teaspoon freshly ground black pepper

1 rotisserie chicken, meat removed and diced or shredded

1 teaspoon freshly squeezed lemon juice

Grated Parmesan cheese, for topping

1. Preheat the oven to 350°F and prepare a 9 x 13-inch baking dish with cooking spray.

2. Bring a large pot of water to boil for the bucatini, then add in the Better Than Bouillon®. Cook the pasta according to the package directions; drain and set aside.

3. In a sauté pan, melt the butter over medium heat. Sauté the onion and mushrooms until the onion is translucent and the mushrooms are mostly cooked through.

4. Add in the flour and stir. Let cook for at least 1 minute.

5. Add in the chicken broth, half-and-half, Velveeta®, salt, and pepper. Stir to combine.

6. Once Velveeta® has fully melted, add in the diced or shredded chicken, lemon juice, and cooked pasta. Stir to fully combine.

7. Using tongs and a large spoon, transfer the mixture into the prepared 9 x 13-inch baking dish. Top with grated Parmesan cheese, as much as desired.

8. Place in the oven and bake for 30 to 45 minutes, or until lightly browned on top.

9. Serve hot and enjoy!

PREP TIME: 25-30 minutes | BAKE TIME: 30-45 minutes

6 cups chicken broth

1 pound ham bone (leave some of the meat on the bone)

1 (14.5-ounce) can diced stewed tomatoes

1 cup chopped Vidalia onion

1 cup chopped celery

1 cup chopped baby potatoes

1 cup chopped carrots

1 (8-ounce) can tomato sauce

½ cup shredded cabbage

½ cup frozen corn kernels

½ cup canned cut green beans

¼ cup long grain rice

¼ cup finely broken dry spaghetti

1 garlic clove, minced

2 tablespoons granulated sugar

2 teaspoons Better Than Bouillon® ham base

¼ teaspoon freshly ground black pepper

Kosher salt, to taste

JONES' OLD FASHIONED VEGETABLE SOUP

{SERVES 10 TO 12 }

A simple and heartwarming soup with all the delicious vegetables, this is best enjoyed on a chilly winter day. Throw everything in the pot and let it cook!

1. Add all ingredients to a large stock pot set over medium-high heat.

2. Bring to a boil and boil for 30 minutes.

3. Reduce the heat to low and simmer the soup for 2 hours, stirring occasionally.

4. Season with salt.

5. Serve hot. Freeze any leftovers in an airtight container.

PREP TIME: 35 minutes | COOK TIME: 2 hours 30 minutes

AMARETTO CHEESE BALL

{SERVES 16 TO 20}

This cheese ball is so festive and makes a fabulous presentation, especially on a charcuterie board. This spread on a gingersnap with a slice of prosciutto is fantastic.

———

1. Mix the first three ingredients in the bowl of a stand mixer fitted with the paddle attachment.

2. Cover and place the bowl in the refrigerator to chill. Chill for at least 1 hour.

3. Once chilled, remove from bowl and form into a pinecone shape. Garnish by placing the toasted almonds all around the outside of the pinecone-shaped ball. You can choose to use pine needles on top of the cheese ball if you want to give it a more realistic appearance.

4. Serve with Anna's® Ginger Swedish Thins or Lotus® Biscoff cookies.

PREP TIME: 15-20 minutes | CHILL TIME: 1 hour

16 ounces cream cheese, at room temperature

½ cup confectioners' sugar

1 ½ teaspoons almond extract

Whole toasted almonds, as needed

Anna's® Ginger Swedish Thins or Lotus® Biscoff cookies, for serving

BROCCOLI AND CAULIFLOWER GRATIN

{SERVES 6 TO 8}

This side dish comes together quickly, which is great for Christmas time with busy schedules. The Dijon-style mustard adds a great tang, while the red pepper adds just the slightest kick of heat.

---

1 ½ pounds broccoli florets

1 ½ pounds cauliflower florets

Cooking spray

Kosher salt, to taste

Freshly ground black pepper, to taste

2 ¼ cups mayonnaise

2 cups grated cheddar cheese

6 green onions, sliced

3 tablespoons Dijon-style mustard

¼ teaspoon ground red pepper

4 tablespoons dry Italian bread crumbs, plus more for topping

1. Steam the broccoli and cauliflower florets until crisp and tender, about 10 minutes. Drain well.

2. Preheat the oven to 350°F and prepare a 3-quart casserole dish with cooking spray.

3. Arrange the steamed florets in the prepared casserole dish. Season with salt and pepper.

4. In a medium mixing bowl, stir together the mayonnaise, cheese, green onions, mustard, ground red pepper, and bread crumbs.

5. Spoon the mayonnaise mixture over the florets. Sprinkle with additional bread crumbs over the top.

6. Bake for 25 to 30 minutes and serve warm.

PREP TIME: 15 minutes | COOK TIME: 35-40 minutes

PORK CROWN ROAST WITH CHESTNUT PEAR STUFFING

{SERVES 10 TO 12}

A Christmas main dish that will wow everyone at the dinner table! Be sure to check with your butcher ahead of time to make sure they will have the large pork loin available. You'll use many of the same veggies for the pan sauce and the stuffing; these can be prepped at the same time. Remember to plan for an additional 30 minutes for the pork to rest before serving.

---

1. In a large sauté pan with tall sides, add the bacon, and cook over medium heat. Let the bacon get brown and crispy.

2. Add the celery, onions, and fennel and season with salt. Cook the vegetables until they get soft and very aromatic, 8 to 10 minutes. Add the rosemary and garlic and cook for 1 to 2 minutes more.

3. Toss in the chestnuts, dried cranberries, and pears, and stir to combine. Add the wine and let it reduce by half over medium-low heat.

4. Put the bread in a large mixing bowl and add the cooked vegetable mixture to the bread. Stir to combine and douse the bread with half of the chicken stock. Use your hands to combine the bread, vegetables, and stock. Add more chicken stock if needed to really saturate the bread. Season with salt to taste and set aside.

5. Preheat the oven to 450°F.

6. In a small bowl, combine the garlic, rosemary, sage, and crushed red pepper with the olive oil. Sprinkle the pork generously with salt and brush both sides with the olive oil herb paste.

PREP TIME: 45 minutes | BAKE TIME: 3 hours 45 minutes

CONTINUED ON NEXT PAGE

CHESTNUT PEAR STUFFING

8 ounces slab bacon, cut into ¼-inch dice

4 ribs celery, cut into ¼-inch dice

2 Vidalia onions, cut into ¼-inch dice

¼ fennel bulb, cut into ¼-inch dice

Kosher salt, to taste

4 sprigs rosemary, leaves removed and finely chopped

3 garlic cloves, smashed and finely chopped

8 ounces peeled chestnuts, coarsely chopped

¾ cup dried cranberries

4 Anjou pears, peeled and cut into ¼-inch dice

2 cups dry white wine

12 cups cubed crustless, stale sourdough

4 cups chicken stock, warmed and divided

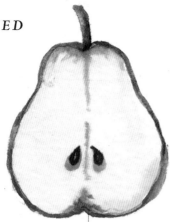

PORK

4 garlic cloves, smashed and finely chopped

1 bunch fresh rosemary, leaves removed and finely chopped

1 bunch fresh sage, leaves removed and finely chopped

½ teaspoon crushed red pepper flakes

½ cup extra-virgin olive oil

Kosher salt

1 (13-rib) pork loin, membrane between the rib bones slit to allow the pork to curl around and stand up

Chestnut and Pear Stuffing, (page 189)

PAN SAUCE

3 cloves garlic, smashed

2 ribs celery, cut into ¼-inch dice

1 Vidalia onion, cut into ¼-inch dice

½ fennel bulb, cut into ¼-inch dice

8 cups chicken stock, divided

2 cups dry white wine

2 bay leaves

Kosher salt, to taste

Freshly ground black pepper, to taste

PORK CROWN ROAST WITH CHESTNUT PEAR STUFFING

7. Place the pork in a large roasting pan and stuff the center with the Chestnut and Pear Stuffing. Place the leftover stuffing in a baking dish and set aside to cook once pork is finished.

8. For the pan sauce, place the garlic and diced veggies around the pork. Add half the chicken stock, the wine, and the bay leaves to the pan. Sprinkle everything with salt.

9. Cover the pork bones with aluminum foil to prevent the bones from burning. Place the pork in the oven. Roast until the pork is starting to brown, about 30 minutes.

10. Turn the oven down to 325°F and roast for another 2 ½ hours, basting occasionally with the pan sauce. Rotate the pork a couple of times during the cooking time. If the liquid level reduces, replace it with the remaining stock.

11. When the pork is cooked to the proper doneness—an instant-read thermometer should read between 140° and 145°F —remove it from the oven. Carefully transfer to a serving platter and cover it loosely with aluminum foil. Let it rest for 20 to 25 minutes. Turn down oven to 350°F and bake leftover stuffing, if desired, for 35 minutes.

12. Transfer the pan juice to a small saucepan and bring to a boil. Lower the heat to allow the sauce to simmer, taste, and add more salt and pepper if needed. Remove from heat, and blend the veggies with an immersion blender, if desired, to create a smoother sauce.

13. To serve, scoop out the stuffing and cut the pork between the bones to create chops. Top with pan sauce.

BEEF STROGANOFF

{SERVES 4 TO 6}

This is one of my favorite go-to dinners, especially for those chilly winter nights. It is a classic that the whole family will always enjoy.

———

1. Flatten the steaks to about ⅓-inch thick with a meat mallet.

2. Slice the steaks into strips, cutting any excess fat, and season with salt and pepper.

3. Heat 1 tablespoon vegetable oil in a large skillet over high heat and scatter half of the beef in the skillet, moving it quickly with tongs. Cook for about 30 seconds per side to brown. Transfer to a plate and set aside.

4. Heat the remaining tablespoon of oil, repeat with the remaining beef, and transfer to the plate.

5. Lower heat to medium, then add the butter to the skillet. Add the onions and cook for about 1 minute. Add in the mushrooms and cook until the onions are golden in color and the mushrooms have softened.

6. Scrape the bottom of the pan to get all the golden bits up, then add the flour and cook while stirring for about 1 minute.

7. Add half of the broth while stirring, and once incorporated, add the remaining broth.

8. Add in the sour cream, mustard, and Worcestershire sauce. Don't worry if the sour cream looks split, as it will continue to melt and incorporate.

9. Bring to a simmer and allow to thicken about 3 to 5 minutes. Season with salt and pepper to taste.

10. Add the beef along with the juices on the plate to the skillet and simmer for 1 minute.

11. Remove from the heat and serve with egg noodles or pasta of your choice. Top with chopped chives and enjoy!

PREP TIME: 10-15 minutes | COOK TIME: 15-20 minutes

2 pounds boneless ribeye steak

Kosher salt, to taste

Freshly ground black pepper, to taste

2 tablespoons vegetable oil, divided

3 tablespoons unsalted butter

1 Vidalia onion, thinly sliced

10 ounces button mushrooms, sliced

2 tablespoons all-purpose flour

2 cups beef broth

⅔ cup sour cream

1 tablespoon Dijon-style mustard

½ teaspoon Worcestershire sauce

8 to 10 ounces pasta or egg noodles of choice, cooked according to package directions

Chopped chives, for garnish

LEMON CHEESE LOGS

{MAKES 15 DOZEN COOKIES}

A delicious cookie to add to the Christmas cookie lineup. The prep time is a little longer than most recipes, but the "wow" factor makes these worth the effort. Santa will love them.

———

1 cup granulated sugar

1 cup (2 sticks) unsalted butter, at room temperature

3 ounces cream cheese, at room temperature

1 large egg yolk

2 ½ cups all-purpose flour

½ teaspoon kosher salt

1 cup finely chopped pecans

½ teaspoon freshly grated lemon peel

6 ounces semi-sweet chocolate morsels

1. In the bowl of a stand mixer, combine the sugar, butter, and cream cheese. Cream until light and fluffy, about 3 minutes.

2. Add in the egg yolk and beat well.

3. In a small mixing bowl, add the flour and salt. Whisk to combine.

4. Slowly add the flour mixture into the mixer and mix well. Remove the bowl from the mixer.

5. Add in the chopped pecans and grated lemon peel. Stir by hand until evenly distributed.

6. Cover and chill the dough in the refrigerator for 1 hour.

7. While the dough is in the refrigerator, preheat the oven to 325°F. Line half-sheet pans with parchment paper. If using a convection oven, decrease the temperature to 300°F.

8. After an hour, remove the chilled dough from the refrigerator. Pinch off a dough ball the size of a nickel and roll into a log 1 ½-inches long. You can get 30 cookies to a half-sheet pan. Using a fork, press down ⅛ inch to make grooves in the dough. (Dip the fork in a bowl of ice water as needed.)

9. Place cookies in the oven and bake for 18 to 20 minutes, or until crispy and lightly browned. Let cool slightly.

10. Melt the chocolate morsels and transfer to a shallow bowl. Dip the end of the cooled cookie in chocolate and refrigerate to set completely before serving or storing.

NOTE: Half of the dough can be frozen to bake off at another time.

PREP TIME: 1 hour | CHILL TIME: 1 hour
BAKE TIME: 18-20 minutes

CREAM CHEESE BRAIDS

{MAKES 4 BRAIDS}

This recipe requires plenty of time—chill time in the refrigerator overnight as well as a second rise of 1 hour before baking—so make sure to read through the entire recipe before beginning. When the recipe calls for "scalded" sour cream, it means to heat an ingredient to the point just before boiling. I love to make this recipe for friends and family. Each cheese braid serves 4 to 6 people.

---

1. Scald the sour cream by placing it in a small saucepan over medium heat. Let the sour cream heat up and start to bubble around the edges. Remove the pan from the heat before the sour cream begins to boil.

2. Transfer the scalded sour cream into the bowl of a stand mixer fitted with the paddle attachment. Add the sugar, margarine, and salt. Mix well and let cool slightly.

3. In another large mixing bowl, dissolve the yeast in warm water. Let the yeast sit for 10 minutes, or until foamy.

4. Stir the activated yeast mixture into the sour cream mixture. Add in the eggs slowly, mixing well after each addition.

5. Gradually add the flour and mix until it comes together (dough will be soft).

6. Cover the bowl tightly and chill in the refrigerator overnight.

7. After chilling for at least 12 hours and before removing dough from the fridge, make the filling. Mix the softened cream cheese, sugar, egg, vanilla, and salt using an electric mixer. Set aside.

8. Line baking sheets with parchment paper and retrieve dough.

9. Divide the dough into fourths, using a sharp knife or bench scraper. Turn each portion out onto a heavily floured surface and knead 4 or 5 times.

10. Roll each piece of dough into a 12 x 8-inch rectangle.

PREP TIME: 45 minutes | RISE TIME: 1 hour
CHILL TIME: 12 hours | BAKE TIME: 15-20 minutes

8 ounces sour cream

½ cup granulated sugar

½ cup (1 stick) margarine, at room temperature

1 teaspoon kosher salt

2 (¼-ounce) packages active dry yeast

½ cup warm water (using an instant read thermometer, it should be between 105° to 115°F)

2 large eggs, beaten

4 cups all-purpose flour, plus more to cover kneading surface

FILLING

16 ounces cream cheese, softened

¾ cup granulated sugar

1 large egg, beaten

2 teaspoons pure vanilla extract

⅛ teaspoon kosher salt

GLAZE

2 cups confectioners' sugar

¼ cup whole milk

2 teaspoons pure vanilla extract

CONTINUED ON PAGE 208

SPAGHETTI WITH CLAM SAUCE

{4 SERVINGS}

As a preteen, I would visit my sister Bitsy and her husband, Jeff, during the summer. The 10-year age difference had me spellbound by her mastery in the kitchen. This was one of the first entrées I perfected. It's delicious!

———

¼ cup extra-virgin olive oil

2 to 3 garlic cloves, minced

½ cup fresh parsley, chopped

⅓ cup sliced black olives

1 (10-ounce) can baby clams

1 box spaghetti noodles

Freshly grated Parmesan cheese, as desired, for topping

1. Heat the oil in a heavy-bottomed pan set over medium heat. Sauté the garlic and parsley until the garlic becomes fragrant and is slightly brown, about 2 to 3 minutes.

2. Add in the olives and clams, including the juice from the clam can.

3. Simmer until heated through, about 7 to 8 minutes.

4. While sauce is simmering, measure out as much spaghetti as desired for 4 servings, then prepare according to package directions.

5. To serve, toss sauce with spaghetti noodles and top with freshly grated Parmesan.

PREP TIME: 10-15 minutes | COOK TIME: 10 minutes

HOT PARMESAN DIP

{ 1 ½ - Q U A R T   C A S S E R O L E   D I S H }

Parmesan, mushrooms, and sun-dried tomatoes…a delicious combination! This dip is easy to prepare and would be a great addition to a charcuterie board. If you are looking to add it to your charcuterie board, use small individual ramekins instead of a 1 ½-quart casserole dish. Heat each ramekin as needed and place on the board with crackers or toast rounds.

---

1. Preheat the oven to 325°F and prepare a 1 ½-quart baking dish lightly with cooking spray.

2. Combine all ingredients in a mixing bowl and mix thoroughly.

3. Place the Parmesan mixture in the prepared baking dish and heat in the oven until hot and bubbly, about 20 minutes.

4. Serve hot with toast rounds or crackers.

*NOTE: If you don't have premade toast rounds, slice Italian bread into ½-inch rounds, then toast in the oven at 325°F until golden brown. Cool and store in plastic resealable bags.

PREP TIME: 15 minutes | BAKE TIME: 20 minutes

Cooking spray

1 cup Hellmann's ® mayonnaise

8 ounces sour cream

1 cup grated Parmesan cheese, packed

½ cup thinly sliced green onions

½ cup sliced button mushrooms

½ cup sun-dried tomatoes, drained, patted dry, and chopped

Toast rounds or crackers for serving

CHAMPAGNE CHICKEN

{ SERVES 6 TO 8 }

I learned early on in catering that if the dish sounded more sophisticated, it might justify a higher price! This was a classic in our catering division and will be a favorite for your family.

———

4 tablespoons unsalted butter

12 ounces sliced button mushrooms

4 green onions, sliced

1 tablespoon freshly squeezed lemon juice

2 cups plus 2 tablespoons all-purpose flour, divided

1 tablespoon Better Than Bouillon® Roasted Chicken base

1 teaspoon kosher salt

¾ cup water

1 ½ cups half-and-half

¾ cup (or more if desired) champagne

6 to 8 chicken breasts

2 large eggs

1 cup whole milk

2 tablespoons Morton® Nature's Seasons

2 tablespoons extra-virgin olive oil

1. Melt the butter in a medium sauté pan set over medium heat and sauté the mushrooms until tender, about 5 to 7 minutes.

2. Add in the green onions and lemon juice. Stir to combine and reduce heat to low to keep warm.

3. In a small bowl, combine 2 tablespoons flour, Better Than Bouillon®, kosher salt, and water. Stir to combine.

4. Turn the heat to medium-low. Pour the flour mixture into the pan, stirring constantly until warmed.

5. Add the half-and-half, and cook until thickened, stirring constantly. Pour in the champagne and cook until heated through. Turn the heat down to low while you prepare the chicken breasts.

6. Preheat the oven to 350°F and line a sheet pan with foil or parchment paper.

7. Using a meat mallet, pound each chicken breast to ¾-inch thickness.

8. In a shallow bowl, mix the eggs and milk. In a separate shallow bowl, mix the remaining 2 cups of flour and Nature's Seasons®.

9. Dip the chicken breasts in the dry mixture, then the wet mixture, and then dip again in the dry mixture, shaking off any excess. Repeat until each has been coated.

10. Heat olive oil in a separate sauté pan set over medium heat. (Add more if needed to cover the bottom of the pan.)

11. Pan fry each chicken breast for about 3 to 4 minutes per side. You are looking for a quick fry to brown the chicken breasts.

12. Place the browned chicken breasts in a large casserole dish. Pour the champagne sauce over the chicken and bake for 20 minutes, or until a thermometer inserted in the middle of the chicken reads 165°F. The sauce will thicken as it cooks.

13. Remove the casserole dish from the oven and serve immediately. Enjoy!

PREP TIME: 10-15 minutes | COOK TIME: 45-50 minutes

LITTLE ROSEMARY AND HONEY BISCUITS

{MAKES 18 TO 20 BISCUITS}

The quickest biscuits to prepare for the Christmas table. Using a miniature muffin pan creates the perfect size for these biscuits. Plus, the children can help put the dough in the muffin pan. I love the flavor combination of rosemary and honey!

1 cup self-rising flour

1 tablespoon chopped fresh rosemary

⅓ cup cold unsalted butter, cut into small cubes

8 ounces cream cheese, softened

1 tablespoon plus 1½ teaspoons honey

1. Preheat the oven to 400°F and have an ungreased miniature muffin pan at the ready.

2. Combine the flour and rosemary in a large bowl. Cut in the butter with a pastry blender until crumbly. (You can also use a fork or your fingers.)

3. With an electric mixer, beat the cream cheese and honey at medium speed until creamy. Add in the flour mixture; beat at low speed just until the dry ingredients are moistened.

4. Spoon the dough into the miniature muffin pan, filling each section to the top.

5. Bake for 14 to 16 minutes, or until golden brown. Serve warm.

PREP TIME: 20-25 minutes | BAKE TIME: 14-16 minutes

MUSHROOM CASSEROLE

{ SERVES 8 }

Allowing this casserole to sit overnight lets the bread crumbs soak up all the flavors and the extra bread crumbs on top give it a great crunch. Add this casserole to the Christmas table for a new side that the entire family will love. This recipe was made famous by the First Lady of Georgia, Mary Beth Busbee, in her book, *Mary Beth's Sampler: A Georgia Cookbook*. It originated in Chris Lambert's kitchen in Madison, Georgia.

---

1. Prepare a large casserole dish with cooking spray.

2. In a large skillet, melt the butter over medium heat. Sauté the sliced mushrooms until mostly cooked through. Remove from heat and place the mushrooms in a large mixing bowl.

3. Place half of the bread crumbs in the bottom of the prepared casserole dish.

4. To the mixing bowl, add the onion, celery, green bell pepper, mayonnaise, salt, and pepper. Mix well to combine, then pour the mushroom mixture over the bread crumbs in the casserole dish.

5. In a small mixing bowl, stir together the eggs and milk. Pour egg mixture over the top of the casserole. Top the casserole with the remaining bread crumbs, cover, and refrigerate overnight.

6. When ready to serve, preheat the oven to 350°F.

7. Remove the casserole from the refrigerator and uncover. Pour the cream of mushroom soup over the top of the casserole.

8. Bake for 50 minutes. With 10 minutes remaining, sprinkle the grated Swiss over the top.

9. Remove from the oven and serve warm.

Cooking spray

2 tablespoons unsalted butter

1 pound fresh button mushrooms, sliced

8 slices white bread, crust trimmed and crumbled, divided

½ cup chopped Vidalia onion

½ cup chopped celery

½ cup chopped green bell pepper

½ cup mayonnaise

1 teaspoon kosher salt

½ teaspoon freshly ground black pepper

2 large eggs

1 ½ cups whole milk

1 (10.5 ounce) can cream of mushroom soup

1 cup grated Swiss cheese

PREP TIME: 25-30 minutes | BAKE TIME: 50 minutes

POTATOES AU GRATIN
{MAKES 9 X 9-INCH CASSEROLE DISH}

A simple and classic side dish to add to your family's meals. The kids will love these cheesy potatoes!

1½ pounds baking potatoes (about 2 potatoes)

Cooking spray

½ cup shredded Swiss cheese, divided

½ cup shredded Gruyère cheese, divided

½ cup grated Parmesan cheese, divided

1 cup heavy cream

1 teaspoon kosher salt

½ teaspoon freshly ground black pepper

2 tablespoons unsalted butter, melted

1. Wash the potatoes and slice about ⅛-inch thick using a mandoline. Submerge the potato slices in a bowl of water.

2. Preheat the oven to 350°F and prepare a 9 x 9-inch casserole dish with cooking spray.

3. Arrange a layer of potatoes in the bottom of the casserole dish and sprinkle with the three cheeses. Continue layering potatoes and cheeses until you've used them all, ending with a layer of cheese.

4. In a separate bowl, whisk the heavy cream with the salt and pepper. Pour the cream mixture and the melted butter over the potatoes.

5. Place in the oven and bake for 1 hour, or until golden brown on top.

6. Let stand for about 10 minutes before serving. Serve hot.

PREP TIME: 25 minutes | BAKE TIME: 1 hour

FRENCH ONION STUFFED PORK LOIN
{SERVES 6}

This is a delicious recipe to check off the "pork" aspect of the New Year's Day meal. The nice part is you can make this recipe the day before.

---

1. Preheat the oven to 450°F.

2. In a large cast iron skillet (or other oven-safe skillet) set over medium-high heat, melt the butter.

3. Add the onions and ½ cup beef broth; cook until the onions are browned and tender, about 15 to 20 minutes. Transfer the cooked onions to a bowl and tent with aluminum foil to keep warm.

4. Butterfly the pork loin. Placing the pork on a cutting board, hold a knife blade parallel to the board and carefully make a lengthwise cut about ⅓ of the way from the bottom of the pork, being careful not to cut through. Stop cutting about 1 inch from the other side of the pork.

5. Open the pork loin like a book.

6. Cover the entire cut of meat with plastic wrap and pound to an even ⅓-inch thickness.

7. In a small bowl, combine the oil, salt, pepper, and Italian seasoning. Rub mixture over both sides of the pork loin.

8. Top the inside of the pork loin with half of the cooked onions and one cup of the shredded cheese. Cover with a layer of the Black-Eyed Pea Salad.

9. Tightly roll the pork loin to completely enclose all the fillings. Using kitchen twine, tightly secure the roll.

10. In the same skillet that you cooked the onions, set over medium heat, add the pork loin to the pan and sear on all sides, about 5 minutes each side.

3 tablespoons unsalted butter

2 Vidalia onions, thinly sliced

1 cup beef broth, divided

1 center-cut pork loin, about 3 pounds

2 tablespoons extra-virgin olive oil

1 teaspoon kosher salt

¼ teaspoon freshly ground black pepper

1 teaspoon Italian seasoning

2 cups shredded Gruyère cheese, divided

½ cup Black-Eyed Pea Salad (page 209)

Fresh flat-leaf parsley, as garnish

PREP TIME: 25 minutes | BAKE TIME: 55-65 minutes

CONTINUED

CONTINUED
FROM PAGE 207

FRENCH ONION STUFFED PORK LOIN

11. Pour the remaining ½ cup beef broth over the loin.

12. Transfer the skillet to the oven and cook for 25 to 30 minutes, or until a thermometer inserted in the middle of the pork loin reads 145°F. Occasionally baste the pork loin with the pan juices.

13. Remove the skillet from the oven and set the oven to broil. Place the remaining cheese and onions on top of the pork loin and place back in the oven to cook for about 5 minutes, or until the cheese is melted and golden brown.

14. Remove the pork loin from the oven and let rest for 5 to 10 minutes before slicing.

15. Slice and garnish with parsley, if desired.

CONTINUED
FROM PAGE 195

CREAM CHEESE BRAIDS

11. Spread a quarter of the filling over each rectangle, leaving a ½-inch margin. Roll the dough up in jelly roll fashion, starting with the long side.

12. Pinch the edge and ends together and place on the prepared baking sheets.

13. Make 6 "X-cuts" across the top of each roll.

14. Cover and let rise in a warm place (70 to 80°F) for about an hour.

15. Thirty minutes before baking, preheat the oven to 375°F.

16. Bake for 15 to 20 minutes, or until the tops of the braids are lightly browned.

17. While the braids are baking, prepare the glaze. In a mixing bowl, combine the confectioners' sugar, milk, and vanilla extract. Whisk until a smooth glaze comes together.

18. Remove from the oven and let cool completely on the pan.

19. Spread the glaze over each braid. Serve or wrap in plastic wrap and aluminum foil to store in the freezer for future use.

BLACK-EYED PEA SALAD

{SERVES 6 TO 8}

This recipe is so colorful. It certainly plays into the tradition of eating black-eyed peas for New Year's, but you'll find ways to use it all year.

———

2 cloves garlic, minced

½ cup rice vinegar

⅓ cup extra-virgin olive oil

¼ cup freshly squeezed orange juice

½ teaspoon Dijon-style mustard

Kosher salt, to taste

Freshly ground black pepper, to taste

2 (15-ounce) cans black-eyed peas, drained and rinsed

1 small red bell pepper, diced

1 rib celery, diced

1 large carrot, peeled and diced

2 green onions, sliced

½ bunch fresh cilantro, finely chopped

1. In a small bowl, combine the garlic, vinegar, oil, orange juice, mustard, salt, and pepper. Mix until well combined into a dressing.

2. In a separate bowl, pour in the black-eyed peas, bell pepper, celery, carrot, green onions, and cilantro. Stir to combine.

3. Pour the dressing over the black-eyed peas mixture and stir to combine.

4. Cover the salad and refrigerate for 8 to 10 hours.

5. Serve cold. This is also used to stuff and garnish the French Onion Stuffed Pork Loin (page 207).

PREP TIME: 20-25 minutes | CHILL TIME: 8-10 hours

Pictured on page 206

HOT MUSHROOM DIP

{MAKES 2½ CUPS}

I bet I've made this hundreds of times! My recipe for this goes back to the early '80s, but my guests and clients still rave about it. If you have any leftovers, it's great on a steak hot off the grill.

---

4 slices thick, center cut bacon

2 tablespoons reserved bacon drippings

2 tablespoons unsalted butter

½ pound fresh mushrooms, sliced (crimini, button, or portobello)

1 medium Vidalia onion, finely diced

1 clove garlic, minced

2 tablespoons all-purpose flour

¼ teaspoon kosher salt

⅛ teaspoon freshly ground black pepper

8 ounces cream cheese, cubed

2 teaspoons Worcestershire sauce

1 teaspoon soy sauce

½ cup sour cream

Crackers or toast points, for serving

1. Cook the bacon in a large, high-sided skillet over medium heat.

2. Once cooked, remove and crumble the cooked bacon into small pieces. Set aside crumbled bacon and 2 tablespoons of drippings.

3. Heat the reserved bacon drippings and the unsalted butter in a large high-sided skillet over medium heat.

4. Sauté the mushrooms, onions, and garlic until the mushrooms have softened and the onions turn translucent. Cook until most of the liquid has evaporated.

5. Stir in the flour, salt, and pepper.

6. Add in the cubed cream cheese, a few cubes at a time, until melted. Then stir in Worcestershire and soy sauce. Finally, stir in the sour cream and bacon pieces. Stir constantly until the mixture is incorporated.

7. Continue to cook over medium-low heat until heated through. Transfer to a small casserole dish and serve with crackers or toast points.

PREP TIME: 10-15 minutes | COOK TIME: 15-20 minutes

ROASTED BRUSSELS SPROUTS SALAD WITH APPLE CIDER VINAIGRETTE

{SERVES 6}

Shaved Brussels sprouts make an excellent salad with all the delicious sweet and salty ingredients mixed in. This is one of my new favorites, introduced on my show as an exceptional side dish.

Cooking spray

2 pounds Brussels sprouts, washed and root ends trimmed

Extra-virgin olive oil, as needed

Kosher salt, to taste

Freshly ground black pepper, to taste

½ cup Candied Pecans, broken into pieces (from *The VeryVera Cookbook: Recipes from My Table*, page 60)

¼ cup dried cranberries

6 ounces cooked thick cut bacon, very finely chopped

½ cup crumbled goat cheese

APPLE CIDER VINAIGRETTE

1 garlic clove, minced

1 small shallot, sliced

¼ cup apple cider vinegar

2 tablespoons freshly squeezed lemon juice

2 tablespoons honey, plus more as needed

1 tablespoon Dijon-style mustard

⅓ cup pecan oil

Kosher salt, to taste

Freshly ground black pepper, to taste

1. Preheat the oven to 425°F and line two large, rimmed sheet pans with parchment paper or foil greased with cooking spray.

2. In the bowl of a food processor, shred the Brussels sprouts using the slicing attachment. If you do not have a food processor or slicing attachment, slice the sprouts by hand, very thinly.

3. Divide the sliced Brussels sprouts between the two baking sheets and spread into an even layer. Drizzle both sheet pans with olive oil, salt, and black pepper. Toss to combine.

4. Place the pans in the oven and roast for about 20 minutes, or until the Brussels sprouts are browned and tender.

5. Remove from the oven and set aside. Let cool to room temperature.

6. While the Brussels sprouts are cooling, mix together the vinaigrette.

7. Add all ingredients to a blender, except for the oil, salt, and pepper. Blend to dissolve the honey.

8. Once the honey is dissolved, slowly pour in the pecan oil while the blender is mixing on low.

9. Add salt and pepper to taste; adjust the sweetness level by adding honey if needed. For the best flavor, allow the vinaigrette to rest for at least 30 minutes to let the flavors blend.

10. Once cool, place the brussels sprouts in a large mixing bowl. Add in the pecans, dried cranberries, and bacon pieces.

11. Shake the vinaigrette to blend and add to the mixing bowl. Combine well and serve immediately, topped with crumbled goat cheese.

PREP TIME: 30 minutes | COOK TIME: 20 minutes

DARK CHOCOLATE
VINAIGRETTE

{MAKES 1 CUP}

A fun way to incorporate chocolate into every part of the Valentine's Day meal! The special dark has the right amount of sweetness and bitterness to use in a vinaigrette. This recipe is truly a perfect choice for Valentine's Day with red berries, candied almonds, and chocolate.

¼ cup Hershey's® special dark chocolate, chopped

¼ cup balsamic vinegar

1 ½ teaspoons honey

¼ teaspoon kosher salt

⅛ teaspoon freshly ground black pepper

¼ cup extra-virgin olive oil

1 (5-ounce) box spring mix

½ cup sliced strawberries

½ cup candied almonds

1. In a microwave-safe bowl, melt the chocolate in 20-second intervals and stir until smooth.

2. Whisk in the vinegar, honey, salt, and pepper.

3. Slowly drizzle in the olive oil while whisking.

4. Toss spring mix, strawberries, and candied almonds in a large bowl.

5. Drizzle the dressing over the salad right before serving.

*NOTE: Any remaining vinaigrette can be stored in an airtight container in the refrigerator for up to two weeks. The salad dressing may start to separate but can be whisked until it becomes uniform again.

PREP TIME: 10 minutes

GRILLED CABBAGE AU GRATIN
{SERVES 4 TO 6}

A delicious mix of cabbage, gooey cheese, and spices to add to the table on some of the coldest days. Grilling the cabbage wedges adds another layer of flavor, an extra step that you don't want to skip. Make sure to serve hot along with your favorite entrée and warm bread.

---

1 pound cabbage, sliced into wedges

Cooking spray

¼ cup finely grated Parmesan cheese

¼ cup plain bread crumbs

2 tablespoons extra-virgin olive oil or unsalted butter

1 leek, trimmed, halved lengthwise, and chopped

2 large eggs

1 cup heavy cream or whole milk

¾ cup freshly shredded Swiss or Gruyère cheese, divided

¼ cup all-purpose flour

1 teaspoon kosher salt

¼ teaspoon freshly ground black pepper

½ teaspoon caraway seeds

⅛ teaspoon ground cardamom

Pinch grated nutmeg

1. In a large grill pan, or directly on the grill, cook the cabbage wedges. Grill for about 2 to 3 minutes per side; you are looking for grill marks and a quick cook.

2. Remove the cabbage wedges to a cutting board and slice thinly into ribbons. Place the shredded cabbage in a bowl and set aside.

3. Preheat the oven to 375°F and prepare a 2-quart baking dish with cooking spray.

4. Dust the dish with the Parmesan cheese and the bread crumbs.

5. Set a large sauté pan over medium heat and add the 2 tablespoons of olive oil or butter. Once the oil is hot or the butter has melted, add the chopped leek and sauté until tender, about 3 to 5 minutes.

6. Add in the shredded cabbage and sauté until cabbage is tender and most of the liquid has cooked off.

7. Meanwhile, in a large mixing bowl, whisk together the eggs, heavy cream or milk, ½ cup of the cheese, flour, and seasonings. Mix well.

8. Remove the cooked cabbage and leek mixture from heat and add it to the mixing bowl with egg mixture. Stir to combine.

9. Pour into the prepared baking dish and cover the top with the remaining ¼ cup cheese.

10. Place in the oven and bake for 40 to 50 minutes or until golden on top. Serve hot.

PREP TIME: 25 minutes | COOK TIME: 40-50 minutes

SOUR CREAM AND ORANGE COFFEE CAKE

{SERVES 12}

A moist coffee cake that is large enough to feed a crowd. The streusel is in the middle of the coffee cake and sprinkled on top, so there is plenty of flavor and texture. This cake is a delicious combination of chocolate and orange flavors.

1. In a medium bowl, whisk the brown sugar and cinnamon to blend.

2. Add in the butter and rub it with your fingertips until the mixture holds together in small, moist clumps.

3. Mix in the pecans and chocolate chips.

4. The streusel can be made up to 3 days ahead. Cover and refrigerate until ready to use.

5. To make the cake, preheat the oven to 350°F and prepare a 9 x 13-inch baking pan with baking spray.

6. Sift the flour, baking soda, and baking powder into a medium bowl.

7. In the bowl of a stand mixer, beat the granulated sugar and butter until blended and smooth.

8. Beat in the eggs, one at a time, mixing well after each addition. Add in the grated orange peel and vanilla extract.

9. Mix in the sifted flour mixture in 4 additions alternating with the sour cream, beginning and ending with the flour mixture.

10. Stir in the orange juice by hand and combine well.

11. Spread half of the batter in the prepared pan. Sprinkle with half of the streusel.

12. Drop the remaining batter over the streusel in heaping tablespoonfuls. Carefully spread the batter to make an even layer.

13. Sprinkle with the remaining streusel.

14. Bake the cake for 30 minutes.

15. After the first 30 minutes, lay a sheet of foil loosely over the pan to keep the topping from browning too quickly. Continue baking about 35 minutes longer, or until a knife or toothpick inserted into the center of the cake comes out clean.

16. Cool the cake in the pan, placed on a cooling rack, for 20 minutes. Dust the top with confectioners' sugar; serve warm or at room temperature.

NOTE: The cake can be made 2 days ahead of time. Cool completely and store in an airtight container at room temperature.

PREP TIME: 25 minutes | BAKE TIME: 1 hour 5 minutes

STREUSEL

1½ cups firmly packed light brown sugar

1 tablespoon ground cinnamon

6 tablespoons salted butter, diced

1½ cups coarsely chopped pecans

1 cup semi-sweet chocolate chips

CAKE

Baking spray

3 cups all-purpose flour

1½ teaspoons baking soda

1½ teaspoons baking powder

1⅓ cups granulated sugar

¾ cup (1½ sticks) salted butter, at room temperature

3 large eggs, at room temperature

1½ teaspoons freshly grated orange peel

1½ teaspoons pure vanilla extract

1½ cups sour cream, divided

¼ cup freshly squeezed orange juice

Confectioners' sugar, as topping

VERA'S FAVORITE POT ROAST

{SERVES 6 TO 8}

Need something to have the house smelling great when the children get home from school? Always worked at my house!

———

Cooking spray

1 (3 to 4 pound) chuck roast, preferably bone-in

1 (2-ounce) envelope Lipton Onion Soup Mix®

1 (10.5 ounce) can cream of mushroom soup

2 to 3 carrots, peeled and cut into 1-inch pieces

10 ounces button mushrooms, quartered

1 or 2 large Vidalia onions, quartered

½ head of cabbage, cut into large wedges

3 stalks celery, cut into 1-inch pieces

3 to 4 tablespoons all-purpose flour

½ cup water

1. Preheat the oven to 325°F and prepare a roasting pan covered with foil or Dutch oven with cooking spray.

2. Place the roast in the prepared baking dish and season all sides with the onion soup mix.

3. Spoon the cream of mushroom soup on top of the roast.

4. Distribute the prepared and cut vegetables in the pan around the roast.

5. Cover and bake for 3 to 4 hours, or until fork tender.

6. After cooking, remove the pan from the oven. Ladle the cooking juice into a small saucepan.

7. In a small bowl, mix the flour and water to make a slurry.

8. Set the saucepan over medium-low heat, and slowly add in the slurry mix, as much as desired, to thicken into a gravy. Cook for at least 2 to 3 minutes.

9. Serve the gravy over the pot roast.

PREP TIME: 25-30 minutes | COOK TIME: 3-4 hours

SHRIMP AND GRITS

{SERVES 4 TO 6}

A dish that is a love letter to the South, perfect for Valentine's Day! There is nothing quite like a bowl of comfort food shared at the table with friends and family.

---

1. Cook the grits according to package directions. After the grits have finished cooking, add the salt, butter, and some half-and-half, depending on your preference for the grits' consistency. Set aside, covering to keep warm.

2. In a large mixing bowl, season the shrimp with the Tony Chachere's® and Cajun seasonings. Set aside.

3. In a large sauté pan, add the olive oil and sauté the diced onion for 2 to 3 minutes over medium heat. Add in the minced garlic and cook for another minute, or until fragrant.

4. In a liquid measuring cup, combine the heavy cream and chicken broth and stir.

5. Pour the chicken broth mixture into the pan with the onions and garlic. Cook for 3 minutes.

6. Add the shrimp and andouille sausage to the pan. Cook for 3 to 4 minutes, or until the shrimp begins to curl and turn pink.

7. To serve, place the grits on the bottom of a dish and top with the shrimp mixture, making sure to ladle some of the sauce on top as well. Top with shredded cheese and green onions, if using.

PREP TIME: 20 minutes | COOK TIME: 15-20 minutes

2 cups uncooked quick "5-minute" grits (not instant)

½ teaspoon kosher salt

4 tablespoons unsalted butter

Half-and-half (optional)

2 ½ pounds medium (36/40) raw shrimp, peeled and deveined

1 ¼ teaspoons Tony Chachere's® Creole Seasoning

3 ½ teaspoons Cajun seasoning

1 tablespoon extra-virgin olive oil

⅔ cup diced Vidalia onion

2 ½ teaspoons minced garlic

⅓ cup heavy cream

1 ¼ cups chicken broth

10 ounces andouille sausage, cut into half-moon slices

Shredded cheddar cheese, optional

Sliced green onions, optional

HOT POTATO CLASSIC

{ SERVES 12 }

Do you love a twice-baked potato? How about all the flavor and not all the work? This is a super easy side dish to serve with steak and a salad.

Cooking spray

1 large (3-pound) package frozen hash browns, slightly thawed

2 cups sour cream

2 cups shredded sharp cheddar cheese

1 (10.5 ounce) can cream of chicken soup

½ cup unsalted butter, melted

½ cup chopped Vidalia onion

1 teaspoon kosher salt

1 teaspoon freshly ground black pepper

1. Preheat the oven to 350°F and prepare a 9 x 13-inch pan with cooking spray.

2. Spread the hash browns in the bottom of the pan.

3. In a separate large mixing bowl, mix the sour cream, cheddar cheese, cream of chicken soup, butter, onion, salt, and pepper.

4. Pour the sour cream mixture over the hash browns in the baking dish.

5. Place the pan in the oven and bake for 1 hour. Serve hot and enjoy!

PREP TIME: 10 minutes | BAKE TIME: 1 hour

OATMEAL LACE COOKIES
{MAKES 32 TO 36 COOKIES}

This is by far my husband's favorite cookie. These cookies get their name from their lace-like appearance. The recipe has been adapted over the years and now I'm confident that it's just right!

1 cup Quaker Oats® Old Fashioned Oats

1 cup granulated sugar

1 ½ teaspoons all-purpose flour

¼ teaspoon kosher salt

½ cup (1 stick) salted Land O Lakes® butter

1 large egg, lightly beaten

1. Preheat a convection oven to 325°F and prepare three cookie sheets with aluminum foil, dull side up. For a conventional oven, preheat to 350°F. Use the center rack and cook one pan at a time.

2. In a medium mixing bowl, combine the oats, sugar, flour, and salt. Stir well.

3. Place butter in a small saucepan set over medium-low heat and melt until almost bubbling.

4. Pour the hot butter over the oats mixture in the mixing bowl. Stir until the sugar is completely dissolved.

5. Add in the beaten egg, stirring vigorously until the mixture is thick, about 1 minute.

6. Drop the cookie mixture in scant teaspoonfuls at least 2 inches apart on the cookie sheets.

7. Place the sheet pans in the oven and bake for 10 to 12 minutes, or until the edges are browned and the centers are golden. Watch carefully in the last 5 minutes, the cookies bake very quickly.

8. Remove the pans from the oven and let the cookies cool for about 1 minute on the pan before transferring the foil to a cooling rack. Let the cookies cool completely before trying to remove them from the foil.

NOTE: For sweet and salty caramel flavor, sprinkle the warm cookies with kosher salt.

PREP TIME: 20 minutes | BAKE TIME: 10-12 minutes

Pictured on page 79

JONES' CRANBERRY SALAD

{SERVES 10}

A perfect side dish that is almost dessert-like! Using lemon Jell-O®
helps cut through some of the sweetness of the orange-cranberry
mixture. Make sure to plan ahead and prepare this early.

1. Pulse the cranberries, orange segments, and orange zest in a food
   processor until broken up.

2. Pour the cranberry mixture into a medium bowl and stir in the
   granulated sugar. Let sit at room temperature for 1 hour.

3. After 1 hour, add in celery and pecans. In a separate bowl, add the
   Jell-O® mix and stir in the hot water to dissolve. Add in the cold
   water and mix well. Add the dissolved Jell-O® to the cranberry
   mixture and stir to combine.

4. Pour into a 9 x 12-inch casserole dish. Cover and refrigerate until
   set, preferably overnight.

PREP TIME: 30 minutes | CHILL TIME: 1 hour, plus overnight to fully set

1 pound cranberries

2 navel oranges, segmented

Zest of ⅓ orange

1 cup granulated sugar

1 cup chopped celery

1 cup chopped pecans

1 (6-ounce) box Lemon Jell-O®
mix

3 cups water (2 cups hot and
1 cup cold)

LAMB CHOPS WITH MUSTARD CRUST

{SERVES 4}

This recipe was very popular at wedding receptions in the late '90s. If we could find the baby lamb chops, we would include that as a passed item and call them lamb popsicles with pesto sauce.

Cooking spray

2 cups fresh white bread crumbs

2 large garlic cloves, minced

4 teaspoons minced fresh rosemary

4 teaspoons minced fresh thyme

6 tablespoons Dijon-style mustard

3 pounds rack of lamb

Kosher salt

Freshly ground black pepper

SAUCE

2 cups beef broth

¼ cup (½ stick) unsalted butter, softened

¼ cup pesto, for topping

1. Preheat the oven to 400°F and prepare a rimmed sheet pan with cooking spray.

2. In a small bowl, mix together the bread crumbs, garlic, and fresh herbs.

3. Rub the mustard all over the rack of lamb, covering both sides. Coat the rack with the bread crumb mixture and season with salt and pepper. Repeat until all lamb has been coated and seasoned, then transfer the rack to the prepared sheet pan.

4. Place the pan in the preheated oven and cook for 35 to 40 minutes, or until a thermometer inserted into each chop reads 145°F. Remove lamb from pan, reserving drippings, and set aside to rest.

5. While the lamb is resting, make the sauce.

6. In a large saucepan, heat the beef broth and add in the pan drippings. Bring the mixture to a boil and cook until the broth mixture is reduced to ½ cup.

7. Whisk in the butter and mix thoroughly.

8. Once sauce is completed, slice the lamb into chops and divide into 4 servings.

9. To serve, pour the sauce over the lamb chops and drizzle each chop with pesto.

PREP TIME: 25 minutes | COOK TIME: 35-40 minutes

DARK CHOCOLATE
BALSAMIC ROASTED CARROTS

{SERVES 4}

Carrots seem to be the forgotten vegetable, but this recipe and presentation is terrific for a gorgeous plate or a platter on a buffet. The bitter dark chocolate pairs perfectly with the balsamic vinegar, which becomes sweet when it reduces.

1. Preheat the oven to 375°F and line a rimmed sheet pan with parchment paper.

2. Wash and dry the carrots, then place on prepared sheet pan and spread in a single layer. Drizzle the carrots with the olive oil and sprinkle evenly with salt. Lay the thyme sprigs on top.

3. Place the pan in the oven and roast until the carrots are tender and brown in spots, about 35 minutes. During cooking, shake the pan periodically and rotate at the halfway point so the carrots cook evenly.

4. While the carrots are cooking, make the reduction sauce.

5. Pour the balsamic vinegar in a small saucepan set over medium-low heat. Simmer until the vinegar has reduced by half. Remove the pan from heat and add in the chocolate. Let the chocolate melt for 30 seconds, then gently stir the sauce until the chocolate has melted completely and the sauce is smooth. Add the honey and salt and mix well. Cover the pan to keep the sauce warm until you're ready to serve the carrots.

6. To serve, discard the thyme and arrange the carrots on a serving dish. Drizzle generously with the reduction sauce, and serve immediately.

7. Any remaining reduction sauce can be stored in an airtight container in the refrigerator for up to 2 weeks. The sauce will need to come to room temperature on the countertop before warming slightly.

PREP TIME: 15 minutes | COOK TIME: 35 minutes

1½ pounds carrots (about finger-width thick), with green tops, peeled and trimmed to about 1 inch

1½ tablespoons extra-virgin olive oil

¾ teaspoon kosher salt

3 sprigs fresh thyme

REDUCTION SAUCE

½ cup aged balsamic vinegar

¼ cup roughly chopped Hershey's® Special Dark Chocolate

½ teaspoon honey

Generous pinch kosher salt

CHOCOLATE CHIP CHEESE BALL

{MAKES 1 CHEESE BALL}

A Valentine's Day dessert for the entire family. This cheese ball actually tastes like chocolate chip cookie dough and is delicious with the graham crackers. Although the cheese ball mixes up quickly, be sure to plan for the refrigeration time.

8 ounces cream cheese, at room temperature

½ cup (1 stick) unsalted butter, at room temperature

¼ teaspoon pure vanilla extract

¾ cup confectioners' sugar

2 tablespoons light brown sugar

¾ cup miniature semi-sweet chocolate chips

¾ cup finely chopped pecans

Graham crackers or animal crackers, for serving

1. Beat the cream cheese, butter, and vanilla extract in the bowl of a stand mixer fitted with the paddle attachment until fluffy.

2. Gradually add in both sugars, beating until just combined.

3. Stir in the mini chocolate chips by hand. Cover the bowl with plastic wrap and refrigerate for at least 2 hours.

4. After 2 hours, shape the cheese mixture into a ball and wrap again in plastic wrap. Refrigerate for at least another hour.

5. Place the finely chopped pecans in a pie dish. Before serving, roll the cheese ball in the pecans. Serve with graham crackers or animal crackers.

PREP TIME: 15 minutes | CHILL TIME: 3 hours

CHOCO-LATTE LAYER CAKE

{MAKES 20 TO 24 SLICES}

Our February Cake of the Month in our mail-order division, this cake was a customer favorite.

———————

1. Preheat the oven to 325°F. To prepare 3 (9-inch) pans, first coat with baking spray, then line with parchment paper, and finish with a layer of baking spray.

2. Cream the butter and brown sugar in the bowl of a stand mixer fitted with the paddle attachment on medium speed for 5 minutes, or until light and fluffy. Scrape the sides and bottom of the bowl.

3. In a separate mixing bowl, combine the cake flour, cocoa powder, baking soda, and salt and mix with a wire whisk. Combine the coffee and vanilla extract in a separate bowl and mix.

4. Add the eggs to the creamed butter one at a time, beating well after each addition. Then add the sour cream and beat well. Scrape the sides and bottom of the bowl.

5. With the mixer on low, alternately add the flour mixture and the coffee mixture, beginning and ending with the flour mixture. Beat until well blended.

6. Scrape the sides and bottom of the bowl and incorporate any unmixed batter, if necessary.

7. Divide the batter evenly between the 3 prepared pans. Tap the pans on the counter to ensure there are no air bubbles.

8. Bake for 40 minutes. Test doneness by touching a cake top. If it springs back, it is done. If the indentation stays, it needs 2 to 3 minutes longer. Cool the cakes for at least 10 minutes on a cooling rack before removing from the pans. While cakes are cooling, prepare the Choco-Latte Icing.

9. Cream the butter and cream cheese in the bowl of a stand mixer for 3 minutes. At the end of the 3 minutes, scrape the bowl extremely well.

10. Meanwhile, melt the chocolate in the microwave in 20-second intervals until smooth.

11. Slowly add the confectioners' sugar, about 1 cup at a time, beating on low to ensure that the sugar does not fly out of the mixing bowl. After each addition of confectioners' sugar, scrape the bottom and sides of the bowl extremely well.

12. Once all the confectioners' sugar is incorporated, beat on low speed for 3 minutes.

13. Add the melted chocolate, vanilla extract, and coffee granules to the icing mixture and mix on low speed.

14. Spread icing between the cake layers, and then on the top and sides of the stacked layers. Cut into ½-inch or 1-inch slices to serve.

PREP TIME: 30-35 minutes | BAKE TIME: 40 minutes

Baking spray

1⅓ cups unsalted butter, at room temperature

3 cups firmly packed dark brown sugar

3 cups cake flour

1 cup Hershey's® unsweetened cocoa powder, sifted

1 tablespoon baking soda

½ teaspoon kosher salt

1½ cups brewed medium roast coffee

2 teaspoons pure vanilla extract

4 large eggs, at room temperature

1½ cups sour cream

Choco-Latte icing (see below)

CHOCO-LATTE ICING

½ cup (1 stick) unsalted butter, at room temperature

16 ounces cream cheese, at room temperature

1½ cups Hershey's® semi-sweet chocolate chips

2 pounds confectioners' sugar

1 tablespoon pure vanilla extract

2 tablespoons medium roast instant coffee granules

ALMOND OR PECAN COFFEE CAKE

{MAKES 1 (9 X 9-INCH) LOAF}

This is a great neighbor gift for Valentine's Day alongside a great coffee blend. It could also be a nice treat for the office. The recipe can be made with either almonds or pecans— there is no wrong choice!

Baking spray

½ cup (1 stick) unsalted butter, at room temperature

1 cup granulated sugar

2 large eggs, at room temperature

1 teaspoon pure vanilla extract

2 cups all-purpose flour

1 teaspoon baking powder

1 teaspoon baking soda

1 ½ teaspoons kosher salt

1 cup sour cream, divided

FILLING

½ cup chopped nuts (almonds or pecans)

½ cup granulated sugar

⅓ cup firmly packed light brown sugar

1 teaspoon ground cinnamon

1. Preheat the oven to 375°F and prepare a 9 x 9-inch pan with baking spray and parchment paper, allowing some to overhang on the edges. To keep the parchment paper in place, use binder clips to clip the overhang of the parchment paper to the pan.

2. In the bowl of a stand mixer, cream the butter and sugar together until light and fluffy, about 3 to 5 minutes.

3. Add in the eggs, one at a time, beating well after each addition. Add in the vanilla and beat well.

4. In a separate bowl, combine the flour, baking powder, baking soda, and salt. Whisk well.

5. Add the flour mixture into the stand mixer bowl, alternating with the sour cream, beginning and ending with the flour mixture.

6. In another mixing bowl, combine all of the filling ingredients. Mix thoroughly.

7. Pour half of the batter into the parchment-lined baking pan and sprinkle half of the filling over the batter. Repeat with the remaining batter and top with remaining filling.

8. Remove binder clips and bake for 1 hour and 5 minutes, or until a toothpick inserted in the middle of the cake comes out clean.

9. Remove the pan from the oven and place the pan on a wire rack to cool. Once the pan is cool enough to handle (allow 30 minutes or more), use the overhanging parchment paper to lift the coffee cake out of the pan. Let the coffee cake cool completely on the wire rack before storing or slicing and serving.

PREP TIME: 25-30 minutes | BAKE TIME: 1 hour 5 minutes

CHOCOLATE MOUSSE
{SERVES 8 TO 10}

A longtime favorite in our catering division—our family loves it, too!
Individual servings are nice in small ramekins or custard cups. Valentine's
Day is the perfect excuse for over-the-top desserts!

1. Melt the chocolate in the top of a double boiler or on half power in
   the microwave. Remove from heat and let cool slightly.

2. Beat the egg whites in the bowl of a stand mixer with the whisk
   attachment on medium speed. Beat until stiff but not dry. Move the
   whipped egg whites into another mixing bowl and set aside.

3. In the bowl of the stand mixer, beat the heavy cream and sugar with
   the whisk attachment until soft peaks form. Set aside.

4. Whisk the egg yolks in a small bowl and stir into the slightly cooled
   chocolate. The chocolate will get thick but continue to stir until
   smooth. Then, stir in the vanilla extract and kosher salt.

5. Add a spoonful of egg whites and a spoonful of the cream mixture to
   the chocolate to lighten the mixture. Gradually fold in the remaining
   cream and egg whites, leaving the mixture somewhat marbled.

6. Cover and chill for at least 5 hours before serving. Use Pirouette
   Wafers for dipping.

12 ounces semi-sweet or
dark chocolate chips

4 large eggs, separated

2 tablespoons granulated
sugar

1 pint heavy whipping cream

2 teaspoons pure vanilla
extract

⅛ teaspoon kosher salt

Pepperidge Farm® Pirouette
Wafers, for serving

PREP TIME: 20-25 minutes | CHILL TIME: At least 5 hours

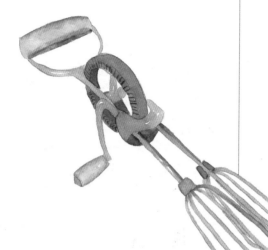

MAMA'S FUDGE

{MAKES 64 (1-INCH) SQUARES}

I'm the middle of five children, and we all called our mother "Mama." When the first grandchild was born, Elizabeth, Mama changed to Mama Bet. It wasn't officially Christmas at our house until this was made. It's truly the best fudge I have ever tasted.

½ cup (1 stick) salted Land O Lakes® butter, plus more for buttering the pan

3 cups granulated sugar

1 (5-ounce) can evaporated milk

Pinch kosher salt

1 tablespoon white vinegar

3 tablespoons light Karo® corn syrup

3 (1-ounce) squares semi-sweet baking chocolate, melted

1 teaspoon pure vanilla extract

½ cup chopped pecans, optional

1. Prepare an 8 x 8-inch baking pan with butter, coating bottom and all sides. Set pan aside.

2. In a heavy-bottomed saucepan set over medium-low heat, lightly brown ½ cup salted butter.

3. Add in the sugar, milk, salt, vinegar, and karo syrup. Stir well to combine.

4. Cook over medium-low heat until sugar mixture begins to boil.

5. Add in the melted chocolate and stir well.

6. Place the lid on the saucepan and let cook over low heat, without stirring, until it forms a soft ball in water. The temperature of the mixture should be between 235°F to 245°F when checked with a candy thermometer. (The lid can be tilted to one side to allow for the thermometer.)

7. Remove the pan from the heat and stir in the vanilla extract and nuts.

8. Place the saucepan in a large bowl of cold water to cool. Beat until ready to spread into the buttered pan. The fudge is ready to transfer to the prepared pan when it begins to thicken, and the chocolate has lost its "sheen." Work quickly!

9. Let fudge cool and set completely before slicing. This is rich, so small, 1-inch squares are appropriate.

PREP TIME: 5 minutes | COOK TIME: 30 minutes

CHAPTER 5

Weddings

I have catered more than 1,000 weddings

in my 40-plus-year catering career. I love weddings, a fascination that most likely started with my mother's wedding album. She got married in June 1940 at her great-aunt Bess's family farm in Jones County, Georgia. As a little girl, I always thought my mother was so beautiful. I was impressed at the beauty of the event: the flowers, the dresses, the pageantry, and, of course, the food.

Here in Augusta, wedding venues range from homes to historic venues—or, like my mother, a working farm with tents and lots of fanfare. And our menus are carefully crafted to fit each unique couple and occasion. No matter the location, I have always enjoyed working with talented event planners, florists, musicians, bands, and lighting experts. Each wedding takes on a life of its own, throwing us curve balls along the way. Some days rain threatens all morning only for the skies to clear and the sun to show up just an hour before the ceremony. Or there are the events where the weather imposes itself like an unwanted guest, never leaving, but no one cares because the wedding is so special and fun. There was even one wedding where the tent was ripped apart by a tornado the night before and another where the power went out right before we were serving hundreds of people. But the show will go on and like our motto reads: "IT WILL GET DONE."

My career has introduced me to many wonderful families, traditions, and unique understandings of protocol and etiquette. I have loved every wedding and the stages of development and planning. But it's always a special privilege when we get to make our favorite dishes for the special day of someone we know and love. The recipes we chose to share in this chapter I made for our VeryVera project manager Rachel Musgrove's wedding at Augusta's historic Medical College building. It was a beautiful, delicious, memorable night filled with plenty of eating, drinking, and dancing, and it was made even more magical because of my veteran staff: Donna Nail, Andrew Jenkins, Julie Voegtlen, and LaWanda Daniels. I truly couldn't pull off these catering events without them.

I hope these recipes will grow with you and your family, as they have with mine, from weddings to baby showers to family reunions to everything in between.

BLOODY MARY SHRIMP SHOOTERS

{MAKES 16 TO 20 (1-OUNCE) SERVINGS}

A traditional favorite, cocktail shrimp sets the tone of a great evening of good food when presented with style. Two smaller shrimp can be used instead of one large, if preferred. A fun appetizer for everybody (these can be non-alcoholic, or you can choose to add vodka).

1. Pour the beer and water in a large pot. Add in the creole seasoning to taste, then add onion rings.

2. Place the pot over medium-high heat and bring to a boil.

3. Once the beer mixture has come to a boil, drop in the shrimp and let cook for 3 to 5 minutes, or until the shrimp turn pink. Once the shrimp have turned pink, remove the shrimp and drop them in an ice bath to stop the cooking.

4. In a large pitcher or mixing bowl, combine the Bloody Mary mix and cocktail sauce. Add in Worcestershire, hot sauce, and creole seasoning.

5. When ready to serve, wet the rim of a shot glass with lemon juice and then dip it on a plate with Tony Chachere's®.

6. Pour 1 ounce of the Bloody Mary mixture into the shot glass. (If you or your guests would prefer, you can also put only cocktail sauce in the shot glasses for a traditional shrimp cocktail appetizer.)

7. To each glass, add desired garnishes. This could be a small piece of celery, olives of choice, or pickled vegetables such as pickled okra or pickled green beans.

8. Top the rim of the glass with the cooked shrimp.

SERVING SUGGESTION: If you would like to make the shooters alcoholic, add ½ ounce of vodka to each shot glass.

PREP TIME: 15 minutes | COOK TIME: 3-5 minutes

SHRIMP

2 (12-ounce) bottles of beer, preferably a lager

12 ounces water

Tony Chachere's Creole Seasoning®, to taste

1 to 2 medium Vidalia onions, sliced in rings

2 pounds extra jumbo (16/20) raw shrimp, peeled and deveined

SHOOTERS

2 cups Bloody Mary mix of choice (I prefer to use ZingZang®)

6 tablespoons cocktail sauce

1 tablespoon Worcestershire sauce

1 teaspoon Texas Pete® hot sauce

Tony Chachere's Creole Seasoning®, to taste (plus as garnish on glasses)

Freshly squeezed lemon juice, as needed

Celery, optional

Olives, optional

Pickled okra, optional

Pickled green beans, optional

GRILLED FILET OF BEEF WITH GARLIC MASHED POTATOES
{*SERVES 12*}

A delicious meal for any special occasion. Always do as much prep as possible to decrease the time spent in the kitchen during your event. Pare this recipe down and use it as the perfect date night at home!

STEAK SEASONING

1 tablespoon onion powder

1 tablespoon dill weed

1 tablespoon crushed red pepper flakes

1 tablespoon garlic powder

1 tablespoon paprika

1 tablespoon kosher salt

1 tablespoon coarsely ground black pepper

2 teaspoons coriander

GARLIC MASHED POTATOES

5 pounds russet potatoes

1 cup whole milk

6 tablespoons unsalted butter

4 ounces cream cheese

Kosher salt, to taste

Freshly ground black pepper, to taste

6 to 8 garlic cloves, minced

BRUSSELS SPROUTS

Cooking spray

6 pounds Brussels sprouts

Extra-virgin olive oil for roasting

Kosher salt, to taste

Freshly ground black pepper, to taste

---

1. Make the steak seasoning. Combine all spices in a small mixing bowl. Store in an airtight container in a cool, dry place until needed.

2. To prepare the mashed potatoes, peel and quarter the potatoes. Place the potato pieces in a large pot and cover with cold water. Bring to a boil and cook until the potatoes are tender, about 20 to 30 minutes. (The best way to test the potatoes is by stabbing a fork in a large potato piece to see if it is tender enough to mash.)

3. Drain the potatoes and return them to the pot, removed from heat. Mash the potatoes, leaving small chunks if preferred. Slowly add in the whole milk, butter, and cream cheese. Stir until the butter and cream cheese are melted and everything is fully combined. Season with salt and pepper to taste and add in the minced garlic. Cover the pot of mashed potatoes with the lid to keep warm while you prepare the rest of the meal.

4. Preheat the oven to 375°F and lightly grease a sheet pan with cooking spray.

5. Wash and prepare the Brussels sprouts by cutting them in half. Toss the halves in a large mixing bowl with extra-virgin olive oil, kosher salt, and freshly ground black pepper.

6. Place the Brussels sprouts on the pan and bake in the oven for 25 to 30 minutes, or until evenly roasted. While the sprouts are roasting, start preparing the onion rings, red wine reduction sauce, and filets.

7. Heat 1 to 2 inches of vegetable oil in a large skillet until the oil reaches 375°F.

PREP TIME: 30 minutes | COOK TIME: 40-50 minutes

CONTINUED ON PAGE 253

GRILLED PEACH SALAD

{SERVES 8}

This is definitely considered a classic in the summer in Georgia! Grilling the peaches will bring out the sweetness of the stone fruit and the Parmesan crisp on top will be the first wow factor that will have your guests ready to dig in.

---

1. Preheat the oven to 375°F and line a sheet pan with parchment paper.

2. Take ¼ cup of grated Parmesan and place on the prepared sheet pan. Slightly spread the Parmesan out to create a circle. Continue with remaining grated Parmesan, making 8 total.

3. Spray each Parmesan round lightly with cooking spray.

4. Place in the oven and bake for 8 to 10 minutes, or until the Parmesan is crispy. Remove and set aside until ready to serve.

5. Toss the mixed greens with a small amount of the dressing; add more to taste.

6. When ready to plate, place a bed of mixed greens on each plate and top with 3 slices of grilled peaches, 2 slices avocado, 2 grapefruit sections, and top with feta cheese crumbles. Place the Parmesan crisp on top and enjoy!

SERVING SUGGESTION: Offer dressing on the side in case anyone wants to add more to their plate.

PREP TIME: 20 minutes | BAKE TIME: 8-10 minutes

2 cups grated Parmesan cheese

Cooking spray

1 (16-ounce) container mixed greens

Vera's Tomato Vinaigrette (page 102)

24 grilled peach slices (about 4 whole peaches)

16 avocado slices (about 2 large avocados)

16 grapefruit sections (about 1 to 2 large grapefruit)

Crumbled feta cheese, to taste

BAKED CHICKEN BREAST WITH WILD RICE

{SERVES 4 TO 6}

Take the chicken breast to the next level with easy pantry staples. I love the toasted pecans in the rice, not only giving the rice more texture but also adding that toasty, nutty flavor. The gravy on top is the perfect way to make sure each bite of chicken is moist and delicious—and who doesn't love fried okra! Impress all your friends and family with this gourmet meal.

CHICKEN

Cooking spray

4 to 6 boneless, skinless chicken breasts

4 tablespoons unsalted butter, melted (more as needed)

McCormick Montreal Chicken Seasoning®, to taste

McCormick Perfect Pinch Rotisserie Chicken Seasoning®, to taste

Long grain and wild rice blend, cooked according to package directions

½ cup pecan halves

Sliced spring onions, as needed for topping

FRIED OKRA

Vegetable oil, as needed

10 to 12 pieces of whole okra

1 large egg, beaten

¼ cup whole milk

½ cup cornmeal

1 cup all-purpose flour

Kosher salt, to taste

Freshly ground black pepper, to taste

Buttered popcorn seasoning, to taste

CHICKEN GRAVY

2 cups water

2 teaspoons Better Than Bouillon® Roasted Chicken Base

4 tablespoons unsalted butter

¼ cup all-purpose flour

Kosher salt, to taste

Freshly ground black pepper, to taste

1. Preheat the oven to 350°F and prepare a sheet pan with cooking spray.

2. Trim the chicken breasts of any excess fat. Dip each chicken breast in the melted butter and season both sides with equal amounts of McCormick Montreal Chicken Seasoning® and McCormick Rotisserie Chicken Seasoning®, to taste.

3. Place the chicken breasts on the sheet pan and bake for 20 to 30 minutes, or until a thermometer inserted in the thickest part of the chicken reads 165°F.

4. Prepare the long grain and wild rice blend according to the package instructions. While cooking the rice, toast the pecan halves in a dry skillet over medium-low heat. The pecans will get slightly darker in color. Be sure to stir often so the pecans do not burn. After thoroughly toasting, chop the pecans.

5. Add the toasted and chopped pecans to the prepared wild rice. Cover the rice to keep warm while you prepare the rest of the meal.

6. Heat about 1 to 2 inches of vegetable oil in a large skillet to 375°F.

7. To prepare the fried okra, slice the whole okra lengthwise. Mix the beaten egg and whole milk in a small bowl. In a separate mixing bowl, mix the cornmeal, flour, kosher salt, and pepper. Dip the okra slices in the milk mixture, then in the flour mixture, shaking off any excess. Fry the okra pieces in the hot oil until golden brown. Remove the fried okra slices to a paper towel-lined plate. Season each okra slice with the buttered popcorn seasoning to taste.

8. To prepare the chicken gravy, bring water to a boil in a small saucepan (or in the microwave) and mix with the 2 teaspoons chicken base. Remove from the heat.

9. In a separate saucepan over medium heat, melt the butter. Stir in the flour and cook for about 1 minute.

PREP TIME: 25-30 minutes | COOK TIME: 40-50 minutes

CONTINUED ON PAGE 253

BAKED CHICKEN BREAST
WITH WILD RICE

CONTINUED
FROM PAGE 250

10. Slowly add in the chicken stock, continuously stirring until all the liquid is incorporated and the gravy has thickened and is smooth. Taste and season with kosher salt and black pepper, if needed.

11. When ready to plate, spoon the rice in the middle of the plate. Slice the chicken breast and plate it on top of the bed of rice. Pour some of the gravy over the top of each chicken breast and top each chicken breast with the fried okra and sliced spring onions.

GRILLED FILET OF BEEF WITH
GARLIC MASHED POTATOES

CONTINUED
FROM PAGE 246

8. For the onion rings, mix the beaten egg and milk in a small bowl. In a separate mixing bowl, combine the cornmeal, flour, kosher salt, and pepper. Dip each onion ring in the milk mixture, then in the flour mixture, shaking off any excess. Fry the onion rings in the hot oil until golden brown. Remove the onion rings to a paper-towel lined plate and season with salt and pepper.

9. To prepare the red wine reduction sauce, heat the olive oil in a small saucepan over medium heat.

10. Add in the shallots and cook until translucent, about 3 minutes.

11. Pour in the wine and beef stock and reduce the heat to medium-low. Add in the thyme and rosemary and cook until the sauce has reduced by half.

12. Stir in the butter and remove the sauce from heat. Set aside until ready to plate.

13. Prepare the filet of beef by trimming any excess fat. Rub 1 ½ teaspoons of olive oil on the steak, coating both sides. Season both sides of the steak with 1 teaspoon of the homemade steak seasoning.

14. Grill the steak, about 4 to 5 minutes per side, or until desired temperature is reached. Let the steak rest for a few minutes before slicing.

15. When ready to plate, start with the mashed potatoes in the center of the plate. Plate the roasted Brussels sprouts next to the mashed potatoes. Place the sliced filet on top of the mashed potatoes and pour some of the red wine reduction sauce over the top of the sliced steak. Top each steak with a few of the fried onion rings.

ONION RINGS

Vegetable oil, as needed

1 large egg, beaten

¼ cup whole milk

½ cup cornmeal

1 cup all-purpose flour

Kosher salt, to taste

Freshly ground black pepper, to taste

1 to 2 large Vidalia onions, sliced very thinly

RED WINE REDUCTION SAUCE

1 tablespoon extra-virgin olive oil

¼ cup finely minced shallots

½ cup red wine, preferably a cabernet sauvignon or pinot noir

½ cup beef stock

1 sprig fresh thyme

1 sprig fresh rosemary

2 tablespoons salted butter

STEAKS

12 (8-ounce) filets of beef

1½ teaspoons extra-virgin olive oil per filet

1 teaspoon Steak Seasoning per filet (see page 246)

PECAN HAVARTI QUESADILLAS

{MAKES 10 QUESADILLAS}

The buttery and slightly sweet Havarti pairs perfectly with the pecan pieces. This is one of my favorite appetizers, it is light and full of flavor! Serve the quesadilla triangles on a platter with the fig preserves on the side for dipping.

1 (20-count) package of 6-inch flour tortillas

5 cups shredded Havarti cheese

3 tablespoons plus 1 teaspoon chopped pecans

Cooking spray, as needed

Fig preserves, for serving

1. Set a large sauté pan over medium heat.

2. To assemble, take one flour tortilla and top with ½ cup of the Havarti cheese and 1 teaspoon chopped pecans.

3. Top with a second flour tortilla to seal the quesadilla. Spray both sides of the tortilla lightly with cooking spray and place in the sauté pan.

4. Cook until the tortilla is lightly browned, about 3 to 5 minutes per side. Flip over and continue to cook until both sides are lightly browned, and the cheese has melted.

5. Remove the quesadilla from the pan and place on a cutting board. Cut the quesadilla into 6 pieces to serve. Continue making quesadillas with the remaining ingredients. Serve with fig preserves.

PREP TIME: 10-15 minutes | COOK TIME: 6-10 minutes per quesadilla